MW01233568

"Some people want it to happen, some wish it would happen, and others make it happen."
- Michael Jordan

DIAMOND
In The Rough

FROM HUMBLE BEGINNINGS
TO PROMISING FUTURE!

BRANDON MAYE

SPIRIT REIGN
PUBLISHING
A Division of Spirit Reign Communications

Copyright © 2013 Brandon Maye.

All rights reserved. No part of this book may be used or reproduced by any means, graphic, electronic, or mechanical, including photocopying, recording, taping or by any information storage retrieval system without the written permission of the publisher except in the case of brief quotations embodied in critical articles and reviews.

Credit for front cover photo: Personal, N.J Photography Vanita Harris

Interior Page design & layout: Ornan Anthony of OA.Blueprints, LLC

Published by: Spirit Reign Communications

Printed in the United States of America

ISBN: 978-1-940002-00-2 (PB)
ISBN: 978-1-940002-03-3 (HB)
ISBN: 978-1-940002-01-9 (ePDF)
ISBN: 978-1-940002-02-6 (ePUB)

SPIRIT REIGN
PUBLISHING
A Division of Spirit Reign Communications

CONTENTS

DIAMOND IN THE ROUGH · BRANDON MAYE

DIAMOND IN THE ROUGH

A Poem by DanetteKettwich © 2007

I was once a hopeless, lost diamond, concealed in the dark.
In a wretched and dismal cave where,
no light could touch my heart.

The Lord reached in and found, this rough and filthy stone. From
out of the immense darkness, He claimed me as His own.

He set to labor immediately, His love always prevailed.
The reductions made with clarity, using a hammer and three nails.

The cuts were not without, struggle, growth and pain, But with
each came a brighter glow; a new lesson gained.

After the cutting was complete, His brilliance now could shine.
Luminous for all to see, a radiant diamond now refined.

I am far from being flawless; He's perfecting my luster still, This
diamond in the rough, being transformed within His will.

I occasionally become tarnished, I still can find the dirt and grime,
But He always finds and inspires me, once again to shine.

I know someday I will reflect, with His pure and flawless light, In
the radiance and presence of Jesus, the Illuminator of my life.

FOREWORD BY EMMITT SMITH

This story reminds me of myself, just like so many kids in our society today, growing up with the odds against you. It's a great reminder that just because you may be born with things stacked against you it doesn't mean you have to finish that way - the key to life is not how you start but how you end and the journey along the way. Although Brandon may be young he shows an uncommon maturity and I'm proud that he is willing to share his struggle in order to help others and let them know they are not alone.

Brandon's story is not just another football book. Brandon's story is, instead, a story of a young man who displayed a great deal of faith, courage, and determination to inspire others to dream big. As you read this enthralling story you will see why I am so proud of Brandon Maye.

Emmitt Smith, *NFL Hall of Famer*

DIAMOND IN THE ROUGH · BRANDON MAYE

TESTIMONIALS

Without pressure diamonds wouldn't exist and without Brandon's struggles we wouldn't get this Gem of a book. Read it and it will inspire you. - **Jon Gordon, Best-selling Author of The Energy Bus and Training Camp**

The title of the book *"A Diamond in the Rough"* suits him because, though he is rough around the edges, he has the ability to inspire anyone who takes the time to look at the obstacles he has overcome throughout his life. - **Micki Lynn, Bestselling Author, Screenwriter, and Editor**

"Brandon Maye is a true inspiration. He is not only engaging and humble, but he has an intriguing testimony that should be shared with the world. While reading Brandon's book, I cried, I laughed, and I gained a new perspective on a person I am proud to call my friend." - **Raven Magwood, Speaker, Author of "The 7 Practices of Exceptional Student Athletes"**

"Diamond in the Rough" speaks with candor and compassion and is a must read for anyone who has experienced overwhelming disappoint- ment and hardship in their life. The spiritual and emotional journey Brandon Maye takes you on is truly an inspiration, not just to those who have a passion for football or sports, but to all of those who have ever been passionate about the pursuit of their own personal happi- ness. He extends a heartfelt challenge that anyone from any walk of life can embrace." - **Eric Thomas, Author, Motivational Speaker, Entrepreneur**

"I am inspired by B. Maye choosing to put his humbling journey to use by reaching out to encourage many. This book confirms what

I know about him as man of faith, character, and determination. He has the heart of a Lion. I can testify to the validity of his story and relate to it more than others because I grew up in the same area. I had the opportunity to walk the same violent streets that he walked in childhood. Because of his faith and iron will, he chose to not settle for less despite the obstacles he encountered. He worked hard and let nothing get in the way of his dreams. Not only did he excel on the football field, but in life making the best of the hand he was dealt. He also set a great example in the classroom for future student-athletes. We sat together in the Renaissance Hotel and shared thoughts the night after he failed his physical with the Bucs. I knew then that he was not going to stop there. I believe that was the night he was inspired to put his story in a book. I know that my brother's book will serve as encouragement to young children and adults who are on the verge of throwing in the towel on life. His story provides a refreshing gift of hope to me, our community, and the City of Mobile (Prichard)". - **Mark Barron, AP All-American, at University of Alabama, 2012 7th NFL Draft Pick**

"People in the Southeast are passionate about their football. This is a book about a player that grew up amidst that passion. Although the road was not as a clear for him through faith, hard work, and dedication Brandon Maye defeated all the obstacles to survive his rough beginning. He had a dream to become a starter on the football team at a Division 1 college and nothing would stop him. Brandon Maye has a unique story of his journey from Mobile, AL to starting LB at Clemson University, graduating Cum laude, and then playing one season in the SEC at Mississippi State. His story will take you through the ups and downs that a college player faces while try- ing to compete at the highest level, excel academically and mature as a man. I know that you will enjoy this journey as you read the book." - **Dabo Swinney, Clemson University Head Football Coach**

"Young people today face many more challenges than when I was growing up. Brandon Maye has faced many of these difficulties and found that God has helped him meet life's roadblocks head on and be successful. A must read for any person young or older who wants to overcome life's struggles and keep their Godly values intact." - **Tommy Bowden, Former Clemson Head Coach, ESPN Sports Analyst**

"Brandon Maye was one of those kids you enjoyed coaching every day. I met Brandon as he was entering his freshmen year at Davidson High School. It didn't take long to realize that Brandon was a kid with a big heart and big dreams. He told me early and often he wanted to play "Varsity" football. I told him there was not many freshmen around that could help us win on the "Varsity Level." He insisted he was one of those guys. Early in training we timed Brandon in the 40. Sure enough, his forty time reinforced to me he wasn't ready for the "Varsity." I explained to Brandon on numerous occasions as I would drive him home that we needed good freshmen offensive linemen and tight ends. The jersey number he was hoping for on "Varsity" would not happen his first year. His body type and his 40 time was that of an offensive lineman. However, Brandon never stopped dreaming about the "Varsity" and a different position other than what I had selected for him. He worked hard in the weight room and was always ready to talk football (and about a lower jersey number). He wanted to know how he was going to contribute to the team. He truly loved the game and had big goals for himself. His work ethic in the weight room changed his body type and increased his speed and agility. The rest is history as he became one of the nation's best linebackers in college football (with a lower jersey number). He lived his dream, he believed in himself. He had the faith and courage to be different. The world needs more young people like Brandon Maye. - **Glenn Vickery, Head Football Coach, Daphne High School (AL)**

ACKNOWLEDGMENTS

Early in the process I was almost reluctant to write an Acknowledgements page because I feared that I may miss someone. As the project neared completion, that thought quickly changed. It is impossible for me to mention everyone that has had a positive impact on my life, but I dare not forget those who had a direct effect on this book being written and published.

This book would not be possible without the amazing contributions of my editors: former Auburn Women's basketball All-American and Author, Mrs. Loretta Freeman, New York Bestselling Author Mrs. Michelle Burnett. Words cannot express how humbled I am to have not only two outstanding editors, but two amazingly great humans that believed in me and my story.

I have always heard that a child's goals, values, morals, and beliefs start in the household and I can say that statement is true. I am grateful to have parents that have instilled in me the importance of education. They taught me how to be a successful citizen and how to make a difference in this world. I know you probably thought I was losing it when every morning you woke to head to work, I was in the living room writing as the birds chirped and the sun rose in the background. I hope you see now I was on a mission to inspire.I would like to thank Jennifer Johnson for encouraging me throughout the writing process.

The biggest challenge in writing this book was having just had surgery and experiencing incredible amounts of pain as well as being immobile. One thing that was very encouraging to me was the service of my three sisters, Radesha, Iesha, and Adrianna. Whether it was toting my writing materials from the bedroom to the living room or bringing me food and snacks I would not be shocked if you guys still hear the sounds of that bell I rang every time I needed something.

I give a special thank you to all my family and many friends who believed in me as a person and encouraged me to write this book. To my supporters: Ken McElhaney, Ray Lewis, Fran Moore, Stefanie Parker, Connie Streater, Jeff Packer, Ray and Kasey Mahathy, Dan Adams, Loretta Maye, Jennifer Johnson, Uncle Leo, Aunt Sabrina, Debby Laidlaw, Jeff Nelson, Edger McBride, Owen Kink, Vikki Mc-Cartney, Dabo Swinney, Tommy Bowden, Mark Barron, Glen Vickery, Dana , Kellye Whitaker, Mr. Ronnie Gilchrist, Coach Christopher and Kila Rumph.

I want to thank both Clemson and Mississippi State for believing in me as a person and as a player. I am grateful for the memories and the time that I spent with my coaches, teammates, and administrators.

Behind any great story are the people I would like to refer to as prayer warriors. I will like to extend a special thank you to my pastor, Pastor Anthony L. Dixon and First Lady Sandra Dixon, my grandmother, Mrs. Willie Mae May, Elder Bertrand Banks and Evangelist Catherine Banks, Pastor Pearl of Atlanta, Spiritual Mentor Daniel Hall, Mr. Scott Carpenter, Chaplain Tony Eubank, and Jeff Davis.

This project was enhanced by Mrs. Danette Kettwich, who allowed me to use her poem, "Diamond In the Rough" and by the great words written in the foreword by NFL Hall of Fame Running Back Emmitt Smith.

Most of all, I will like to give praise and glory to my Lord and Savior, Jesus Christ, because without His grace and mercy my story would not be a story.

INTRODUCTION

"You should write a book!"

"Your life is a remarkable story of perseverance and determination!"

"Your life is a true testimony and would provide hope and highlight God's mercy!"

These are some of the phrases I've heard throughout my football career, but I never gave it any real thought before now. I always felt I wasn't ready, that I was too young. Would anyone really want to hear my story? However, as I see God's plan through more mature eyes, I decided it was God's time, time for me to tell my story in an effort to show God's mercy and grace. So, welcome to my story... I am Brandon Maye and I am a diamond in the rough.

As I was looking out the window of the airplane, the thought of writing my story came back to me. I wondered where God was leading me. On that plane ride, I began to understand that now may not be the time for me in the NFL, and that God may have a totally different plan for my life than I did. I know that God, in his wisdom, had something much better planned for me. I found peace in the thought that God was positioning me where HE would get the glory and not me. There is a song by Gold City called *Hide Me Behind the Cross* that really fits my situation well and the chorus says, "hide me behind the cross, where my gains become a loss and your glory is in view. Your power will be revealed the more that I am concealed. Hide me behind the cross so the world sees only you." During this time in my life I realized that, perhaps, I was not ready for this particular blessing at this particular time, but that He had other blessings waiting for me. I only had to hold fast to my faith in Him.

It was the spring of 2012, and I had just experienced what some football players only dream of. I had imagined the gigantic Tampa Bay Buccaneers facility and what it would be like to be a part of that organization. By failing my physical however, I was not allowed to participate in the minicamp or take advantage of this opportunity that would have led me to the signing of an NFL contract. I was disappointed, but not broken. The long walk toward the front doors of the Renaissance Hotel seemed to last forever. In the shuttle, feeling lonely and dejected, I could not help but remember my final steps to the glass doors imprinted with the Buccaneers logo. It cut deep into my soul when a player personnel came up to me and said, "good luck with everything" as he collected my playbook. This was just the final blow and the pain of my experience inspired me to write this book.

"Do not grow weary in well doing because in due season you shall reap a harvest." Galatians 6:9

This is a scripture that my mother has shared with me, and I have learned to lean on these powerful words during times of disappointments or times of trials I have had during my life. I want to share my journey in hopes that someone may embrace these written words and find hope in them the way I have.

Before I begin to share my story, let me lay the foundation. This book is not just about football. Football has played an instrumental part in my life and it will be used as a platform for me to talk about God's grace, my faith, and to inspire others who may find themselves in difficult situations. Football is a game that I love and enjoy. Football has opened many doors for me and presented me with many opportunities; however, football does not define me as a person. I have learned many values through the playing of the game, values like faith, determination, teamwork, discipline, and perseverance. Football only lasts for a moment. Determination, values and perseverance however, last a lifetime. Whether it was practices, games, weightlifting, team runs, or training room treatments, those are only temporary. When that moment is over, it is over. At various times in my life, football was the most important part of my life. Now that I'm older I understand that it is not, and will never be, my entire life. I am so much more than a football player, I am God's child. This book tells the journey of my life and the sharing of my faith. I hope reading it will encourage and uplift others. I hope it brings all who read it to a closer relationship with God. It is with God's strength that I made this journey. God allowed me to overcome obstacles, survive disappointments, and destroy generational curses. My prayer is that lives are touched in a special way and people will be filled with hope and encouragement. In essence, it is not about football at all; it is all about GOD.

DEDICATION

This book is dedicated to my parents, Osben and Queen Clark, and grandmother, Willie Mae Maye, for teaching me the morals needed to leave a positive, everlasting legacy.

Also, to those who don't allow their circumstances or what others say they cannot be or do define them, but rather work harder than any human in their industry to make sure failure is not an option.

1

ONCE IN A LIFETIME EXPERIENCE

"Life is a lot like surfing. When you get caught in the impact zone, you need to get right back up because you never know what's over the next wave."

The Soul Surfer, Anna Sophia Robb, 2011

The NFL Draft –Thursday

I got up around 8 am with my mind filled with uncertainty. As I showered and dressed, I was overwhelmed with many thoughts about the events taking place in the next few days. For breakfast I ate the All-Star Special of grits, eggs, bacon and toast at Waffle House. After breakfast, I drove to Encore Rehabilitation to rehab my ankle. A bone spur had been removed from my ankle a month prior to attending Pro-Day at Clemson University on March 8th. Rehab was now an important part of every morning. Molly and Mrs. Tonya, the physical therapists, greeted me at the door when I arrived and immediately started asking me about my feelings on the draft. At that moment I was calm, cool, and relaxed for I believed I had a good understanding about my situation. My agent, Josh, had prepared me with the likelihood of my being called up with a high free agent grade. I remember the sixty-inch plasma TV that hung on the wall near the treadmills. I can still remember how listening to the analysts' voices making predictions about the draft stimulated me. Because of this, I was really pumped up with extra drive this particular day and I worked harder than I ever had before. Throughout my rehabilitation session, my mind again was inundated with various thoughts. I thought about what would happen, how this would bless my family and me financially, and I thought about God's grace in my life as I had overcome multiple injuries and persevered to make it this far.

After my rehabilitation, I met with my friend, Jason Poeth, at Titans Athletics to workout. My intention was to clear my mind of all of the draft drama. Contrary to what I desired, instead of a simple greeting, the first questions out of Jason's mouth were about the NFL Draft. He asked whether or not my agent had contacted me. He asked about the possibilities. He wanted to know where I thought I would fall in the draft and what my draft projection was. I explained to Jason everything my agent told me. I told him that most teams had given me a high priority free agent projection. Jason confidently replied that "all I needed was an opportunity."

I looked over to my right and there was Adrian Cole. Adrian is a McGill-Toolen Catholic Graduate who played football at Louisiana Tech. Adrian was named Sunbelt Conference Defensive Player of the Year in 2011. I joined Adrian and we began warming up for our workout with Jason. The warm-up was intense and focused on explosiveness. We began by building up a good sweat and prepared for a lower body concentrated training regimen. The Titan workouts are always challenging. At Titan, we performed a series of exercises such as squats and Olympic style lifts: snatch, cleans and jerks, and power clings. We completed a series of Tim Tebow rope exercises and concluded the workout with LSU Abs, which are a sequence of grueling abdominal exercises. I was exhausted at the end of the workout and ready to get home to watch the NFL Draft with my family.

On the drive home from Titans Athletics, I listened to gospel music to calm my body and clear my mind. All of the windows were down in my Dodge Charger and I found myself praying and worshipping God for allowing me to get to this point. Once home, I immediately showered to wash the sweat away from the workout. Inside the house, I spoke to family members: Mom Queenie Clark, my dad Osben Clark, my aunt Catherine Banks, my sisters, and others. Before I got in the bathroom to shower, my Grandmother Willie May, gave me a word of inspiration. She was watching TBN in her room and told me to "trust in God and lean not on [my own] understanding." My grandmother is 85 years old and her wisdom, along with my parents', has guided me throughout my life. I showered and put on a tank top and sweat pants. I walked into the living room and greeted everyone. We said grace and sat down to eat baked chicken, mashed potatoes and corn.

Once I was full, I joined my family members who had already gathered in our living area in front of our 60-inch flat screen to watch the first round of the NFL Draft on ESPN. I can still hear the analysts dissecting the various NFL teams' needs, discussions about positions, and football verbiage. As I looked around the room, I found myself looking back on my accomplishments. There is evidence of them all over our living room. I remember looking at my memorabilia hanging on the walls: the life-sized player of the game posters, plaques, framed jerseys, and photographs. I thought about how blessed I was to have achieved so much, despite my humble beginnings. As the draft started and excitement built up in the room, I remember the thrilling moment when NFL Commissioner, Roger Goodell, announced that the draft had officially started. The first pick of the 2012 NFL Draft was Andrew Luck. We continued to watch, knowing that the likelihood of me getting drafted in the first round was unlikely. With every pick, I felt as if I were on a NFL Show. My family analyzed each pick of that night. As the draft neared the end for that night, I begin to grow extremely tired. I later learned from my mom that I had fallen asleep with about ten picks left in that first round.

I woke up Friday morning distracted with anticipation. I was enthusiastic about what could happen this night. This night they would be unveiling the second and third rounds of the NFL draft. I woke up about 9 am and dropped to my knees to perform my routine of early morning prayer. Afterwards, I went to the bathroom to shower and prepared myself for the day. I ate breakfast at my Aunt Catherine Banks' house. My Aunt Catherine lives across town about 20 minutes from my house. Whenever I go to her house, I feel as if I am on a road trip because of the distance and time it takes to get there. My breakfast was the same as the day before. I had grits, eggs, sausage, and toast. I washed breakfast down with a glass filled with Aunt Catherine's specially made punch. After breakfast, I made the long trip back across town to Encore for my rehabilitation session. Rehab sessions on Fridays always seem to be the best because there were not many people around. The solitude and quiet of the Encore Rehabilitation Facility were huge for me during this nerve-racking time. I did not have to answer the basic question that seemed to be asked by each and every person I encountered throughout the draft process: "Do you think you're going to be drafted?" This question somehow emerged in every conversation I had since the end of the season. I would routinely give the reply that my grandma reminded me of often, "If it's of God's will!" Today, I broke my routine. Instead of working out after my rehabilitation session, I went home.

Friday night

Family and friends again gathered in the living area in front of the television to watch the second and third rounds of the NFL Draft. As the draft went on, the likelihood of me getting picked grew along with the excitement of the process. Time passed quickly and, before we knew it, the Third Round was starting. I had watched two former teammates from Mississippi State and Clemson get selected. Fletcher Cox went as a First Round Selection to the

Philadelphia Eagles and Andre Branch went as a Second Round Selection to the Jacksonville Jaguars. My family and I continued to watch as the Third Round ended.

By the end of the Third Round, the house was completely empty except for my parents, grandma, and sisters. As the last selection of that round was made, I walked down the hall towards my room to get in the bed. By this time the whole process was starting to take its toll on me mentally. I was tired and disappointed, but I kept my faith and focused only on the positive. Before going into my room for bed, I poked my head into the door of my grandma's quiet, dark room to say good night. She was sound asleep. The only sounds were those coming from her TV, locked on TBN Gospel channel. I opened my door. The ceiling fan blew heavily creating a cool, calm, peaceful atmosphere in the room. As I lie motionless in the pitch-dark room, I looked out the window to the sky and prayed, *"God please give me favor no matter what route you chose for me in this life. You have been so good to me and I know you wouldn't leave me nor forsake me, AMEN!"*

As I uttered the word Amen, my eyes shut completely and darkness dropped upon my peaceful soul.

Early Saturday Morning
– Reflecting on Momma's example of FAITH

The days seemed to pass faster. I slept until about 3 am. Sleep was what I needed in this chaotic time. At around 6 am, my mom was walking into the front door from her job at Providence Hospital. She had worked a long, hard 13-hour shift as a Registered Nurse. Despite her recent knee operation, she had managed to endure the pain and worked through it to provide for my sisters and me. I mulled over her tireless efforts to make ends meet for us. Her diligence has served as an inspiration in my life, as well as motivation during the most troubling and low times. When things get tough and there are obstacles in my way, I think of the times when she performed incredible feats. My mother went back to school at the age of forty to pursue a degree in nursing. While she was in school without the financial comforts provided by a steady job, she raised four children. I remember it well because it was during the same time period of my red-shirt year at Clemson. I would return home often when the team played away games. I often reflect on one night that I will never forget. I was heading to my room to go to bed and I heard silent cries coming from the den. I cracked the door and looked into the dimly light room. I saw my mom crying. I learned later that she did not have the money she needed to re-take a test that was required for her to gain access into the nursing program. As I think it over now, I know that God provided a way and she was able to take care of it all. The way in which she carries herself is admirable. I believe in her and watched her persevere with dignity, faith, and humbleness. The mental picture I hold of my mother's sacrifices and diligence would serve as a benchmark later in my life. She is the backbone to the whole family and I admire her.

Saturday-the last day of the NFL Draft

Finally Saturday arrived, the last day of the NFL Draft! They would announce the fourth through the seventh rounds. I woke up to the telephone ringing. It was my agent Josh calling to tell me what the game plan was for that day. He assured me that there were several teams wavering over drafting me, which gave me something to hold on to as I went throughout the day. He reminded me that I had suffered an injury and that, because of that injury, there was a lack of production last season. I also had transferred from Clemson to Mississippi State University. The teams still interested in me were the Bengals, Steelers, and the Broncos. I was just praying one of them would give me a shot. Josh also told me that the teams were interested because they saw my versatility. I could play all three of the linebacker positions, I could provide pass coverage and I had the ability to lead the defense. All of these were things I needed to hear, but he also gave me the worstcase scenario as well. He said that if I did fall out of the draft, I would be one of the first to receive a deal as a free agent. This conversation gave me some welcomed encouragement and helped me remember that I needed to keep the faith because, **with God, all things are possible.**

After hanging up the phone, I proceeded with my daily routine. Afterwards, I walked down the hall and stopped by my parents' bedroom. My mom and dad were still asleep but I was just so excited that I woke them up anyway, just to tell them what Josh had said. They too were encouraged by the information. We had all been waiting for this day for so long and words couldn't describe how excited we all were. I was certain that the last three rounds would move at a faster pace than the previous rounds, and that was exactly what I needed. The anticipation was almost overwhelming. My house was full of activity as my mom prepared food again, as she had on the previous nights. Everyone was ready to celebrate and the doorbell was constantly ringing as family members started packing into our small living room. Everyone was waiting to hear my name being called during the NFL draft or, even in the worstcase scenario, that I would get a telephone call from a team signing me as a rookie free agent as soon as the draft was over.

During the earlier rounds, everyone had been firmly camped around the television watching each and every pick, but tonight we just monitored it occasionally. People were walking around, eating and just socializing. Then, in the sixth round, the phone rang. The house grew silent as everyone waited anxiously to see where I would begin my NFL career. We have caller ID on the television and we saw the area code was from Baltimore, Maryland. "I am going to be a Raven," I said to myself as I went to answer the call that would change my life. All of the sudden, that room was filled with excitement. Some family members were screaming and others clapping. The excitement in the room took over like the floods from

Hurricane Katrina in New Orleans. I took a deep breath so I could sound calm in spite of the fact my heart felt as if it were in my throat, and answered the telephone.

All of a sudden, it was like someone kicked me. It was not the Baltimore Ravens calling after all; it was my uncle Leo that lives in Baltimore calling. When I hung up, I had to explain to my family who called. This disappointment only escalated my anxiety. I was now filled with trepidation and it showed. I could see the disappointment I felt mirrored in their expressions. I now felt this huge crush on my chest and cold water in my veins. I had to walk outside to be alone with my thoughts. I have never really been one to express disappointment in front of people so I walked outside and sat where no one in the house could see me. I was filled with uncertainty and doubt. I began to question everything about the last few days. "How could anyone be rated as high as I had been in terms of my position fall so far?" Despite last season and the injuries I had suffered, I had rationalized to myself that I should have been drafted by now. "Is the NFL not the route that God has for me?" I wondered. After sitting on the side of the house for about 30 minutes, I wiped the tears from my face because I did not want to show how crushed I really was and reluctantly walked back into the house.

As soon as I entered, all of my family and friends began consoling me; "You okay?" and "Don't worry" were common that night. The atmosphere in the room went from joyous excitement to cheerless melancholy. It reminded me of the mood of our Clemson football team after the 2009 ACC Championship Game, where we lost in the final drive to Georgia Tech. It was like the air had been sucked out of a balloon around my heart. I knew this feeling very well. This was not the first disappointment or obstacle I had encountered. Though not my cheerful self, my emotions were still very high. I walked into our dining room because the living area was congested with people waiting for me to talk with my agent and see what the plan was. Josh informed us all that, shockingly, no team had contacted him. He also said that throughout the night he and his firm would be aggressively working the phones to find me a new home.

I came out of the dining room a split second after the call to talk to the few people that were still there. The emotions I was feeling were evident despite the fact that I was really trying to hide them. The pain I felt was beyond description, even now. It really was beginning to sink in that my name had not been called during the draft and not one NFL team had called my agent or me. Soon the house was empty and all I could do was be silent in my misery.

The phone rang again around 9 o'clock that night. It was my agent Josh. He was calling again to let us know what was going on. Since I was feeling more than a little dejected, I allowed my mom to intercept the call. She put him on speakerphone so I sat down next to her on the bed. I stayed quiet and listened as she and Josh talked. To be honest, I do not even really remember what was said because it is just a blur to me now. The night had cast serious doubt on my future. Football had been my life for so long; I could not imagine life without it. Questions kept spinning around in my head. Why hadn't any of the NFL teams called me? Was my football career really over? I kept asking myself over and over. The only thing I know for certain is that some point after the call ended, I left my mom's bedroom and got into my car. Where I was going in life or in my car, I had no idea. All I knew for certain was that my life suddenly had no purpose. There was a void in my heart. Football had been an escape from my problems. Football saved me from trouble when I was younger. Football gave me a stage to show my spiritual faith and tell people about God's grace in my life. Football also had given me an opportunity to give the kids in my community hope. I was now facing the reality of no more football.

As I opened my car door, I heard my mom calling out to me. She said, "I know you are hurt. I am too, but don't do anything that will impact your life!"

My disappointment was so great; I didn't want to hear anything that anyone had to say. I just wanted to ride around, get some fresh air and do some real soul searching. I drove around the city of Mobile in silence. I rode for hours as my cellphone rang constantly. I could see the blinking backlights but I really didn't care. I set the cellphone on silent mode and just kept on driving. When I finally looked at my missed calls, I saw that I had missed a lot of calls from my high school sweetheart, Jennifer Johnson. I learned later that, when mom tried to call me but could not reach me, she had called her to have her try to get in touch with me. I know I had everyone worried sick. After what felt like forever, I made a detour from the downtown streets of Mobile and drove over to my old neighborhood on Selmer Street. The street was quiet, and looked dull and lifeless, kind of like I felt at that moment.

All was quiet as I drove around my old stomping grounds to visit places that had been so significant during my life. Selmer Street was the place where people had helped me grow into the man, person and football player that I am today. I also drove by Davidson High, Scarborough Middle, Hillsdale Middle and Phillips Preparatory Academy. I walked into the practice fields alone. I was thanking God for granting me the perseverance and determination that led to my previous successes. After about three hours, I finally decided to head home. I still could not escape the questions going through my mind but instead of answers, all I found was silence.

On my way home, I considered my past. I know that I am blessed beyond measure and these thoughts should never have entered my mind, but they were. I could not focus right then about how God's grace had opened doors for me. All I could focus on was where I was at that moment.

I just could not understand, how could all 32 NFL Teams pass on drafting me, Brandon Maye? How could all 32 teams not even call me about a free agent contract? Why didn't I leave when I was hotter? Why didn't I leave my junior season? Did Josh and his company not work hard enough for me? Could all this be happening because of an ankle injury that I got in pre-season camp at MSU? How could God fail me? I played football for the love of the game. I had high hopes that I could use my talents as a way to repay the Lord, who had been so good to my family and me. I wondered why God was blessing others who played the game for fame and money and not me. I became so depressed while driving back home, I even thought about committing suicide. That is so hard to admit, being a Christian, but that is how I felt at that very second. And my thoughts were not just about me either. I thought about my other failures as well. I believed what I promised my mom at an early age -- I am going to play in the NFL. It was a major let down and a very frustrating moment in my life. I had come so close to realizing my dream and, now that I was not even getting a shot, I was brokenhearted.

When I finally pulled onto Vanderbilt, I was emotionally exhausted. I made my way up the steep hill. I looked over my shoulder and saw an old house that reminded me of something out of a 1970's horror movie. I pulled my car alongside the house and walked up to the front door. All the lights were off and the house now was quiet and somber, which is the exact opposite of what it normally was. Our house was normally filled with people talking and laughing. I was glad that there was nobody in the living room. The last thing I wanted to do was to talk to anyone. As I made my way down the hallway toward my room, the emotions from earlier in the day surrounding the NFL draft were lingering in the house. As I made the final few steps to my room, I could hear movement and light sniffling sounds, almost like someone had a cold. I knew immediately it was my mom. She was still up, weeping and praying for me. She knew how hurt I was and it hurt her knowing how devastated I felt. She knew how much the draft meant to me. This was actually not that unusual. Anytime any of her children were hurting, my mom would fall on her face before God and intercede in prayer for us. Sometimes she would cry all night if one of her children were struggling, hurt or depressed. And if we were out late at night, she would pray for us until we came home, safe and sound. I hated to hear her crying, knowing I caused it by running off like that. I walked towards my room quietly. I just did not want to get upset again. I entered my room and, with tears running down my face, I took off my clothes and lay down on the bed.

My mind just kept right on going, even though all I wanted to do was get some sleep. I started reflecting on my life and how good God had been to me. I thought about how God had showed His favor in my life. I considered how much I had been given and the blessings I had received. God had opened many doors for me and enabled me to touch so many people along the way. Through my testimony, lives had been touched from my hometown in Alabama, all the way to Clemson and Mississippi. I kept thinking about Ecclesiastes 3:1, which states, *"For everything there is a season, and a time for every matter under heaven."*

After lying in my bed for a while, for some reason I decided to turn my phone back on. As soon as I did, I received a call from my pastor since birth, Anthony L. Dixon. Pastor Dixon is the type of pastor that always has a great message for you. He is good at using his troubled childhood and experiences in California as a way to connect to whatever you are struggling with. As he spoke, Pastor Dixon began to minister to my heart. I heard, "The Lord didn't bring me this far to leave me." Pastor Dixon ended his 20-minute message to me by saying not to be discouraged and to just know that whatever happened, "It was God's will!"

After that conversation, I made a decision. I would no longer hold my head low and resolved to not be weary. I chose to trust in God and lean not on my own understanding. I prayed: *"Father, God, I thank you in advance for whatever route you are about to take me in this life. You have been so good to me. From this day forth I will trust in you more. I pray that you give me an even bigger stage to be able to tell my story in relation to your grace. Thank you for giving me strength during those weary childhood nights and surrounding me with a supporting cast. You have installed greatness in me. Now Father I turn my life over to you. From this point forward let your will be done. AMEN."*

As I was ending my prayer, I saw a shadow move across the television that sat near the entrance of my room. The shadow moved closer. Soon, I realized that it was my mother. Despite my efforts to keep quiet she had heard me come in the house earlier, took a moment to gather herself, and had come to my room to check on me. She sat down on the bed and spoke to me in a gentle, soft voice. She asked, "Are you okay? I know you are hurt, but HE (referring to God) is going to see you through!"

Words cannot express the calmness that took over my body as I heard my mother's comforting words. Her faith once again gave me courage and strength. I felt guilty about my selfishness earlier when I walked out, leaving her alone to worry about me and not answering her calls. I know she had waited up all night to make sure that I was all right. I assured her I was and hugged her, as I never had before.

Early the next morning, I received a call from my agent, Josh. He told me that the Tampa Bay Buccaneers and the Eagles wanted to bring me in the next week on a try-out basis to their Rookie Mini Camp. After I hung up, I ran to my parent's room to tell them the news as they were preparing for morning worship service. After disclosing what I initially considered great news, I started my walk back to my room. The devil was playing on my reservations and again I started to question myself. "How am I going to be able to do this?" Two doctors had already diagnosed me as having achilles tendonitis. From what they told me, I had already concluded that the damage may require surgical repair because it was torn. This painful condition, along with the bone spur surgery I had prior to Pro Day, had prevented me from being able to play in any post season All-Star Games and from participating in the NFL Combine. The more I sat in my room thinking about it, the more the pain grew knowing how hard participating in the Rookie Mini Camp would be. I had not run since Pro Day. While at Andrews Institute in Gulf Breeze, Florida, I had a needle procedure as an attempt to alleviate the pain. The doctors there had already informed me that surgery was necessary, but we had decided to take some conservative steps so that I would have some hope of getting a contract signed or being drafted as a free agent. By waiting, I increased the chances of this happening because it allowed my agent to have a much improved negotiating position. Once a deal had been struck, I could sit out during minicamp as I healed from the surgery and be ready for camp. Nevertheless, these conservative measures had not done anything to alleviate my constant pain and now I was going to have to perform during a rookie minicamp after all if I had any chance at all of getting a contract. Finally, I had to resolve that I would just put it in the Lord's hands. I showered, got dressed and went on to church.

Most of that day, I meditated on the message my pastor gave that Sunday morning. He preached on perseverance. It was as if he was just ministering to my heart during his sermon. I was trying to have a positive outlook, but every few minutes, my mind was again inundated with negative thoughts. That is just how the devil works. He plays on your insecurities and tries to shake your faith. I knew this week would be full of rehab and intense, painful training sessions. If I had any hope of performing well, I had to be as prepared as possible. I had three days. I would fly to Tampa on Thursday. I was motivated and worked through the pain for the next three days. But as a consequence of all of this effort, the pain grew increasingly worse and by Thursday, my pain was excruciating and my ankle had swollen severely.

Thursday

On Thursday morning, I woke up to the sound of chirping birds. It was about 6:00 am and I was still tired from staying up late packing everything that I needed for the weekend. I chose to stay in bed just a few more minutes when my aunt, Lisa Jones, walked into my bedroom. She was obviously as anxious as I was.

"B. Maye, wake up!" she balked at me, "you have about 45 minutes before we have to head to the airport!"

My flight was departing at 9:15 that morning and the drive to the airport was only ten minutes. I reluctantly rolled out of bed but I took a personal moment, said a prayer, and thanked God again for waking me up. Then I went to the bathroom to do the typical morning routine. I brushed my teeth, washed my face, showered, and dressed. Just like every other morning, I was dealing with agonizing pain from my Achilles. I made a promise to myself that I was going to beat the odds, in spite of the injury. I had kept reminding myself that I been in this situation before. Prior to leaving for the airport, I told my mom that I was going to compete, no matter what happened or how much pain I was in. I joked around with her and said that someone would have to cut my legs off to prevent me from going.

My aunt, Lisa, drove me to Mobile Regional Airport. Her daughter, Portia Maye, also rode along. The three of us arrived at the airport at 8 o' clock sharp. I quickly got out of the car and headed to the counter to check in at Delta Airlines. I went through the security check and proceeded to the gate. Then, I boarded the plane promptly at 9:00. My connecting flight was in Atlanta. Like always, Atlanta's airport was crowded. There were people moving in every direction in hurried attempts to make it to their flights on time. It kind of reminded me of rush hour in New York City, but instead of cars, with people. Many of my favorite restaurants were available at the airport and, since I had a layover, I decided that I would grab something to eat.

I waited there until they made the announcement that the flight to Tampa was ready to board about an hour later. The plane was one of the larger ones, and it reminded me of all the planes I had flown on when I played at Clemson and Mississippi State when we had to travel to far away games. The flight to Tampa was short, only about an hour and 15 minutes, but I used the time to rest. When I woke up, the sun was beaming through the small side windows of the airplane.

After landing, I made my way to baggage claim and called for the hotel shuttle as I was instructed to do in an email from the Buccaneers Personnel Office that I had received earlier that week. I waited for about 20 minutes, and finally I saw the white shuttle van with the logo for the Renaissance Hotel International Plaza emblazed on the side. I got in and the driver drove me and the other passengers to our destination. The hotel was one the most beautiful places that I had ever seen in my life. As I got out of the shuttle, I was greeted by several of the Tampa Bay Personnel members. They instructed me and a handful of other NFL hopefuls to hurry to our rooms, sit our bags down, and get right back downstairs. We all moved quickly as instructed and returned to the shuttles that waited for us outside. Within minutes, we were heading to their facility, One Buccaneers Place, which is the NFL's largest team facility. As soon as we arrived, we were greeted by several coaches, including Head Coach Greg Schiano. Schiano had been the head coach at Rutgers the year before. He had received a lot of publicity for signing his former player, Eric LeGrand, who had been paralyzed from the waist down in a game the previous season, to a free agent deal. His players obviously meant a lot to him and, I was hoping to be one of those players.

After the greetings were completed, we went to a room where we filled out all the necessary paperwork prior to taking our physical examinations. The physical exams were very different from my high school and college physicals. We went through in-depth EKGs, blood pressure checks, and several other tests. After that, one by one, we went into a room to be examined by their orthopedic doctors. When it was finally my turn to go in, I started to get an uneasy feeling. It was very similar to the feeling I had just a few short days earlier when I was waiting to hear my name during the draft. I did not like it at all and I prayed to God to calm my nerves because I was sure everyone could hear my heart pounding. I walked into the room where three doctors were waiting. They pulled on, poked at and probed every part of my body, or so it seemed. When they got to my ankle, the one on which I had recently had surgery, they looked concerned.

One of the doctors asked, "Why are your Achilles so swollen?"

I answered, "I had seen a doctor and was told it was simply tendonitis."

Trying to fully assess my Achilles injury, the doctors put me through a series of tests. The most terrifying moment was when one of the doctors instructed me to stand up on my toes. After three failed attempts, the three doctors walked outside. I could see them through the glass huddling as if they were calling a play. I knew at that moment that the results would not be good for me. While they talked outside the room, I closed my eyes and tried to calm down. Then they finally returned to the room, with the news that I knew was coming. The amount of swelling in my Achilles was a liability concern for them. I had failed my physical and would not get an opportunity to participate in the camp. I would need reconstructive surgery on my Achilles and, despite my initial disappointment, I counted it as joy. I know that sounds strange but I know God was giving me peace.

I took a little while to walk around the facilities, up and down the corridors of this beautiful place. I was merely thankful to God for allowing me to experience this day. I was happy to have been invited to this NFL facility in spite of my humble beginning.

"A Diamond In the Rough" is originally a metaphor used for the unpolished diamond gemstones that have the potential to become high quality jewels. I identify myself in this term often because it, in essence, describes me. In fact, I have a tattoo on my arm of a diamond in this rough state that serves as a reminder of my hidden potential. Real diamonds go through a cutting process. And, much like a 'rough diamond', I am someone who has hidden, exceptional characteristics and future potential, yet currently I lack the final touches, which will make me stand out from the crowd. At first glance, I seem quite ordinary; yet, my true beauty will only be realized through life's process of cutting and polishing. My journey has taken me through periods of great highs and great disappointments. Through trials and tests of my faith, I feel I have shown perseverance. Through my story, I want to share how I have overcome many obstacles, defeated the naysayers and stunned the haters. My life story is, most importantly, a spiritual journey. I hope that the words on each page can be used to inspire others and that, by sharing my experience; I hope my life can be used as an example to anyone who finds themselves in desperate need of God's touch. This writing is an honest reflection of my life and a challenge for anyone who reads it to trust in God for all they need.

Here I am. I am Brandon Maye. I am a *"Diamond in the Rough."*

2

THE BEGINNING

"We cannot change the cards we are dealt, just how we play."

Randy Pausch, The Last Lecture

Mom's Early Morning Gift

From everything my mother told me about my birth and early childhood, sometimes I am amazed at just how different my life could, or maybe even should, have been. I was a pretty good sized baby and she never ceases to remind me that giving birth to me was a very long and painful experience. She said her emotions and those of my other family members was a mixture of nervousness and excitement as she and the rest of my family eagerly awaited the arrival of my mother's first child, me. When she tells the story, I can just see the doctors and nurses running in and out of my mother's hospital room during her 24-hour labor, trying to keep her as comfortable as possible with various family members coming and going throughout the day. By the way, I am sorry about that mom but, as you taught me, nothing good ever comes easy.

At around 11:00 p.m. on March 27, 1989, family members finally went home to get some rest since they had been at the hospital and cramped in a small room for so long. That just left my mom and dad.

While mom was in labor, my biological father tried to comfort her as best as he could. He would stroke her hands and forehead and tried to offer as much support as he could muster because this was all new to him, too. Even the nurses had given up hope that I would arrive and left to rest. Evidently, I must like to make an entrance because right after they left, guess what? Here I came. I entered this world at 12:01 a.m. on March 28, 1989. I weighed 8 pounds 7 ounces and I was 21 1/2 inches long. Mom said that when she saw how big I was, she knew I would play sports. She said she hoped I played football, which, of course, I did. She was scared about all the contact and the possibilities of serious injuries but those are the risks you take when you play the game.

When my mom held me in her arms for the first time, she cried. Her tears mixed with the sweat already covering her face. At that moment, she said that the book of Genesis came to her. She remembered the scripture where God talks about the pain that woman shall endure at birth. It was right but, she said, it was all totally worth it when she looked at me. After having some alone time to bond with me, she picked up the phone and called family members and friends to share her joy, exclaiming, "It's a boy!" They had all known that for months now. As the sun came up and daybreak dawned, the room again begins to fill with family and friends as they came to look at mom's new bundle of pride and joy.

My biological father, Curtis Berry

Other people have talked to me about my birth and early childhood too. My aunts, Lisa and Cathy, talked to me about the excitement of my biological father, Curtis Berry. They said that the day I was born, he was smiling from ear to ear. I do not remember much about my biological father. He was fatally stabbed when I was only two years old. Though I do not remember him, my aunts always tell me stories about him. They told me that the day after I was born, he picked me up and drove me all around town to show me off. He took me to get my first haircut. Mom did not really like our little adventures because she would be calling everyone to find out if we were all right, where we were, what we were doing and when I would be home. He would make these little trips often so he could share his joy with his friends and loved ones. Mom just worried because she never really wanted me out of her sight for very long. Unfortunately, mom's fears were justified.

One day, my father was making one of his famous detours. He decided that, instead of going home, he would go see his mother, my grandmother. He always worried about her and checked on her often. Several people were hanging out at my grandmother's house when a confrontation took place between her and her current boyfriend. My father stepped in to protect her, and her boyfriend pulled out a knife and stabbed my father in the leg. After stabbing my father, the boyfriend ran out the front door and down the street. My father was a big, brave man. He tried to run after him but this would prove fatal. He was found about 45 minutes later, lying beside a car in a pool of blood. The emergency crews tried to save him, but he was pronounced dead on arrival.

I have heard many other stories about my father over the years. People tell me about how much fun he was to be around and that he was the life of every party. He loved to live life to the fullest. People tell me all the time how much he loved me and how, after late nights of clubbing, he would stand outside of my grandmother's window begging my mom to let him see me. He was also a track star at Williamson High School. I often wish that I had inherited his quickness and speed. My father was talented and had many scholarship offers. He won lots of track events and contributed to several state championship teams as a high school student athlete. Unfortunately, my father made a lot of poor choices that caused him to miss out on so many opportunities. He fell victim to alcohol and enjoyed being the class clown. My mom calls his actions "the generational curse" because my father and his brothers were all alcoholics. Even though I did not really remember my father, I came to understand he was actually a good teacher. His life taught me to never take the same roads he did. I did not want to fall victim to "the generational curse." I did not want to end up lying in a pool of my own blood, on a street, dying. No, I vowed that would not be how my life would turn out.

My dad, Osben Clark

My mom raised me as a single parent from the time I was 2 years old until I turned 4. We lived in Prichard Alabama, a small town near Mobile. My mom faced many challenges since she was raising me as a single parent, and she made many sacrifices to ensure I was well taken care of. Most times, she just did without. After two years of struggling to make ends meet and building a close-knit protectoral shield around me, she met the man that would eventually become my dad. Osben Clark was a mild-mannered Operations Specialist in the United States Navy. He and my mom dated for a while and eventually married. Before meeting my mother, Osben was stationed on the USS Paul FF-1080, a Navy Frigate, and he was there August 2, 1990 when Iraq invaded Kuwait during Desert Shield. Ironically, after transferring to the USS FFG-32, he was sent back overseas and served in Operation Desert Storm, too. He described Desert Storm as one of the most stressful moments of his life. He was concerned about attacks that could come in the night as their ship patrolled the Mediterranean waters.

After returning from overseas, his ship changed home port from Mayport, Florida to home port Pascagoula, Mississippi in January of 1993. In February of that same year, the ship was sent to Benders Shipyard in Mobile, Alabama to undergo repairs. Whenever they entered a new city, Osben and his shipmates would try and find some form of entertainment to temporarily escape the stress of war. Osben asked around town, and he and his shipmates decided to go to a night lounge called the Solid Gold in Mobile, Alabama. This is where he met my mom. Osben moved in with me and my mom in 1994. He brought a firm hand to our family because of the discipline and strict code of conduct he acquired in the Navy. The principles he learned would guide me, along with the values and nurturing provided to me by my mom and grandmother. He helped my mother raise me and my sisters in a rough, peer-pressured environment.

Growing up in Prichard

Our home in Prichard was small, brick, had three bedrooms and had been owned by my grandmother. Our small house would eventually become smaller with the birth of my twin sisters, Lesha and Radesha, quickly followed a year later with the birth of my youngest sister, Adrianna. In addition, several family members moved in as well. There was my cousin who went to school with me at Glendale Elementary. Altogether, there were nine people living under one roof. And that was not counting the people that were always coming and going because my grandma had a kind heart and always wanted to help anyone that was in need. You have no idea how hectic it was at our house on a daily basis.

The small town of Prichard where I grew up was close to the city of Mobile, Alabama.

Mobile is known for its different cultures, sea ports, carnival celebrations-primarily Mardi Gras-and of course sports. It has something that appeals to everyone. There are museums, a symphony orchestra, a professional ballet company. There is historic architecture and it is home to the oldest organized carnival in the United States. Many people believe that Mardi Gras was originated in New Orleans, Louisiana, but it actually was started in Mobile in 1803 by the French Soldiers. However, growing up in Prichard, Alabama was anything but a carnival celebration.

On our small streets, crime is common and there are many negative ways for young people to spend their time. Because of all of the negative pressures in Prichard, many ministers witnessed to me and the other youth in the area at a young age. There were many ministers in my family so this guidance really countered the effects of trouble or peer pressure. My grandma was set and centered on her spiritual beliefs and often she would remind me of how faithful God had been to her. Later, her mentoring and spiritual advice would help me survive some of the hardships, obstacles, and doubts that would come into my life. She worked as a janitor at Dunbar Middle School and she saw every day the problems faced by many people in our local public school system. She saw firsthand how they were not taught to value their education. She made sure my sisters and I knew how important a good education was.

My grandmother also taught me the importance of living for the Lord. She had been saved at a young age and had worked in the church since she was young. Her belief and faith in God has always been an inspiration to me and provided me hope whenever the devil fought me. That was true then and it is still true today. I remember the days when I would walk with her to the EOH Holiness church. We walked because we did not have a car. It was just two streets over from our house, which was located near the projects. It did not matter what the weather was; she never missed a service. Nothing in the world could keep her away from the church and her position-singing soprano in the church choir. I really didn't understand when I was young why she had to go to church every time the doors were open and I didn't understand much about being a faithful Christian when I was young, but I was learning those tenets during those long Sunday morning services. Though the odds were stacked against us, my mom, dad and grandma always would team up to help me whenever I needed spiritual support. This support helped me beat the odds eventually, but I was still young then and had a lot more to learn.

Despite many efforts to lead me in the right direction, I was taken in by the peer pressure and trouble that presented itself in the Prichard community. I can remember my grandma walking out the front door to break up fights between me and other neighborhood children. I still remember when my mom had to quit her job to keep me from getting involved in gang activity and engaging in drug use. Financially, times were hard and soon, my grandma lost her house at 806 Selmer Street. I was then 9 years old and we were homeless. Our family struggled to find a place to live, and fortunately my uncle Sam took us in.

He lived across town in the Toulminville community. We stayed with Sam for two months before moving back to our neighborhood. Another uncle, Sulton, knew a homeowner who was selling their place just down the street from our old house. Our new address was 409 Selmer Street. It was nice to get back to my old neighborhood because we had so many friends and family in the area and it was close for grandma to attend the church she loved. While this took care of the housing issue, it also put me back in contact with kids that were more interested in getting in trouble than attending church.

The house was a small, blue, two-bedroom house that sat back away from the street. We called it the Blue House. Tall trees covered the property. It was not in the best condition, and it reminded me of a box. The house had four rooms and all of the rooms were the same small size. We had a living room, kitchen, and two bedrooms. My parents slept in one of the bedrooms and their king-sized bed took up most of the space. The bathroom was tiny with a green, ancient tub in the corner. The floors were wooden and during the winter season, they could get as cold as any hockey arena floor. In the living room, there was a small, old-fashioned wood heater that had to be lit and tended to during cold nights so the house would have some heat. The forth room was my bedroom. Well, I guess you could say it was not really mine, because I had to share it with six other people. There was my grandma, three sisters, and two cousins that all slept in one full-sized bed. Along the side of the window there sat a small, hard, twin-sized bed. I usually slept alone on that bed unless someone had to stay over. On those nights, I had to share it. Maybe the arrangement was not the most comfortable situation, but complaints were rare because my grandma didn't allow it. She would simply remind us that it was a blessing to just wake up every morning. She often would say, "There are kids in Africa that would want your life." We weren't homeless anymore, but living in this small house taught me gratitude and humility.

As I said before, the location of this house presented another challenge besides cramped living conditions. The house sat next to a pathway that was used as an entrance to the Josephine Allen Projects. From my house, I could look over into the projects and see just next door the drug addicts, alcoholics, and ladies of the night walking by our house all day long. Our yard was dark, overwhelmed by trees and full of trash at times. Since the path was used regularly by people going into and coming out of the projects, my grandma developed relationships with many of them. They would speak as they passed through and some would stop just to say good morning to her. This was not the most positive environment for my younger sisters or me. Prichard City Officials had gone back and forth, trying to get this path covered but all efforts had failed. It was like a path to sin and many destructive things went on just past our yard. Local dog fighters would bring their pit bulls to fight, as people stood around making bets. The winner was decided only after one of the dogs chocked the other one to death. It was cruel and violent, but they always brought in a big crowd. Sometimes the dog fights would end early when the police rushed onto the scene in vain attempts to catch the owners. I saw a lot of dogs just lying dead in the path. This was hard to stomach at first, but after years of watching this take place, I thought it normal. It was just a part of living in the projects of Prichard.

The violence in the community really never seemed to end. Crime and death walked hand in hand and killings were a constant reminder to me that we were never promised tomorrow. I had seen drug deals go bad and one person ending up laying in a pool of blood. Those images will forever haunt me. Break-ins were normal too, so I learned that locking doors was important and I did so every time I left the house. I was not blessed with riches and my family did not have much in terms of finances, yet we valued the little we had and I appreciated everything. Thinking back on our situation, sometimes I have to laugh because we were actually happy even though we were poor.

I often think of those cold winter mornings when the exposed pipes under the house would freeze and burst. I remember those mornings specifically because I would have to go to school without being able to take a bath at home that morning, so I would quickly rush to school before anyone got there and wash up using the bathroom sink. Even though the house was always full of people, there were lonely nights too, when I would lie in bed and toss and turn as I listened to gunshots and police sirens right outside my window. On several occasions, I remember waking up and going outside to find crack heads lying on our front porch. As my parents and grandma fought to make ends meet, there were nights when I went to bed hungry and could not sleep because of the rumbling sounds coming from my empty stomach. In spite of all of this, I never complained because I understood that my parents were working hard and doing their best. I didn't always get what I wanted, but they made sure my and my sisters' basic needs were met. I think back on these times because then, I really thought we were living the good life. I had never known anything different.

I sometimes think about some of the other families that had it worse than us on Selmer Street. Despite my meager upbringing, I always thought we were high class compared to them because I had something that no other kids in the neighborhood had; I had love, support and encouragement from people who cared about my future and worked hard to ensure I had a good one. I had people praying for me constantly and I had role models who taught me grit. The dignity my parents and grandma demonstrated by making the best of situations helped me later during the long, hot two-a-days during my high school and college football careers. The rough environment and humble beginnings would later become my edge. The hardship I endured created a tough, nasty style of playing which I struggled to control at first. Later, I learned to channel those emotions and blossomed as both a player and person.

Although there were obstacles I had faced in my short life, I still found time to have fun both in the neighborhood and at home. In the neighborhood, I would often get together with friends and play sports. There was a big grass field in the middle of the street where we played pick-up football games. This spot would be the place where I learned to love football, the place where I was taught skills by my step dad and park ball coach. The games we played were usually violent and we made contact with no pads. I really think this contributed to my aggressive approach to how I played the game. There would be times when blood was shed and it often ended in a fight. One thing is for certain about the kids on this street; we would fight one day and the next day we would again be playing together, because we knew we only had each other to play with so holding a grudge was pointless. The problems usually started when kids from the projects came on our street and challenged us. This was our field and we were going to defend it. The games usually started with a long period of trash talking between us and them. We defeated the kids from the projects most of the time and, when they lost, they would want to fight. Luckily, we won some of those battles as well. Sometimes we played basketball with these same kids at the Boys and Girls Club located in the projects. There they had the home court advantage and winning at basketball helped keep their win - loss percentage between football and basketball games close to 500.

At home, spending time with family was fun. We would play board games like Trouble, Monopoly, Sorry, and Operation. Love and laughter were good medicine and we took it eagerly to ease the pain of our reality. Spending time together with them definitely made me more family oriented, and despite the size of our house, it was a place we were glad to call home. We made the most of what we had and enjoyed each other. The faith, determination, and persistence of my family paid off too. Three years after first moving into what we called "the blue shack," Osben and my mom bought their first house. It was a remarkable feeling when we moved to West Mobile, away from the violence and negative environment of Prichard. This beautiful, brick house sat down a hill on Vanderbilt Drive and was located across the street from the University of South Alabama. It was a four-bedroom house. My sisters and I now had our own bedrooms. It is funny because, despite having our own rooms, we were so accustomed to sleeping in a crowded room with my grandma and cousins, we felt weird at first. It took some getting used to, and sometimes we would cover the floor of my grandma's room with blankets and stay with her. The toughest part about this move was getting used to the new environment. It was very quiet in our new neighborhood. The sounds of gun shots and sirens were replaced by the chirping of birds or dead silence.

When I reflect on the experiences of those early stages of my life and career, I find that those created within me strength and courage that would get me through the tough times. I have learned to persevere through obstacles while still maintaining my faith in God. Many of the kids I grew up with are still searching for something

DIAMOND IN THE ROUGH · BRANDON MAYE

good and positive in their lives. Looking back gives me strength and courage and I am not afraid to face life's challenges. These challenges are a process we all must go through in order to be refined. They are opportunities to grow and mature.

Despite growing up amidst the violence, poverty and challenges in Prichard then moving to Mobile where crime did abound, sports were a way for me and many other young people to escape. There are high expectations set for people that participate in sports. Mobile County has produced many great athletes that made it out of Mobile and found success in the world of professional sports. These athletes range from Baseball Hall of Famers such as Hank Aaron to athletes like JaMarcus Russell (2007 NFL Draft #1), DeMarcus Cousin (#5th pick in 2010 NBA Draft), Willie Anderson (Future NFL Hall of Famer), and Mark Barron (#7 Pick of 2012 NFL Draft). The list is extensive, proving that some of us actually made it out. But for every one that did, there are sadly many more that had the talent but fell victim to the rough, harsh streets. There are also those forgotten few who were overlooked or not given an opportunity. I just thank God I am one of the ones that had a chance to have a better life.

Family photoshoot in our living room in 2013

Where my spiritual foundation started
EOH Church of Jesus Christ

The house my grandma owned. This is where it all started at.

3

INTRODUCTION TO GOD'S GIFT

"If you can imagine it, you can achieve it; if you can dream it, you can become it."

William Arthur Ward

The year was 1996. Bill Clinton was President of the United States and I was sitting on the floor in front of a small, blurry old-fashioned television set. The picture was not great and our antennae consisted of a silver clothes hanger to get any signal at all. I, with a host of family and friends, was watching Super Bowl XXXL. The New England Patriots were playing the heavily favored Green Bay Packers. There were a lot of football greats playing in that game, including Brett Favre, Desmond Howard, Reggie White, Drew Bledsoe, Curtis Martin, and Willie McGinest. As I sat on the floor watching the game, for some reason I couldn't stop moving. I found myself mimicking the actions of the players in the game. I remember it like it was yesterday. Our house was packed with people. Voices were shouting at the television screen every play. "Run boy Run!" "Make a play!" "Hold them defense!" and "The coach should be fired after this one!"

That Super Bowl was dominated by MVP Desmond Howard and the Packers won 35-12. Many people hung around to see the post-game celebration and trophy presentations. After watching this game play by play and seeing the emotions and excitement of the players, it is safe to say that I had found a new love in the game of football. After all of the people that had filled the living room went home and everybody else at the house headed to bed, I stayed in the living room tossing a football in the air. I watched it spiral down and into my hands and I could visualize myself playing in the big leagues. While I was alone in the dark living room, I dropped to the floor. Up and down I went, doing the most unorthodox form of push-ups anyone has ever seen. I was seven years old and this was the first time I made a commitment to myself that those players on the screen would include me one day. I vowed that I would never allow anyone to outwork me in any endeavor to get there either. At that moment, I convinced myself that you have not worked hard enough until your every muscle and fiber of your body literally aches and you can't move anymore, yet you keep going anyway. So, up and down I went. I continue doing these unorthodox push-ups until I was covered in sweat and my young, weakened muscles could not do anymore. Every night after, I would find a spot on the floor and do push-ups and sit-ups until I could move no more.

Weeks and weeks passed since the night of that Super Bowl game, and my dad was starting to take notice. He saw how determined I was becoming in the game of football. At every party and family event, I had my football in my hands. When my uncle Doug would come over to our house, I would beg him to throw me passes. Because of the size of my hands and my height, I often caught the passes he threw me with one hand over any kid in the neighborhood that dared try to guard me. During Osben's spare time, he took time out to teach me football fundamentals. Gradually he moved on to teaching me specific positions and running me through drills.

It wasn't long before he realized that these few hours he took for me after work every day were paying dividends. They were also keeping me occupied and out of trouble. Osben saw that football was a way of not only keeping me out of trouble, but a way of leading me to a better life. He shared with me his optimistic thoughts. He shared with me his vision that football could open the door for me to get a college education. It had never crossed his mind before that football would lead me to a Division-1 Scholarship, All-American honors, All-Conference honors, and Bachelor's and Master's Degrees. I had never given any serious thought to football or how it would give me a platform to minister to many schools and communities or, how football would later allow me to tell about God's grace and share my testimony with young people.

It wasn't long before Osben started taking more and more time out of his schedule to teach me all about football. On weekends we would leave the hard, cement streets of the neighborhood to the big, grass stadiums in Mobile. We went to Ladd Pebbles Stadium (Home of the Senior Bowl) and to Prichard Stadium (Home of two local high schools, Vigor and Blount). The stadiums provided a more structured atmosphere with fewer distractions so I could concentrate on what he was trying to teach me. Here, there were not cars driving up and down the road with people yelling "Get out of the street!" or people shouting out to friends and other boys hanging around in the street. Here, it was just Osben, me and the pigskin. Needless to say, Osben would sometimes invite other kids along too so we could play. He frequently took advantage of the opportunity to play father figure to them also. This is something that all the kids appreciated and one of the things I love about him.

After a couple weeks of technical and fundamental type training, he took me across town to Rick's Sporting Goods store and bought me my first pair of cleats. Rick and Osben are longtime friends, so he often gave us a discount through my Pop Warner Football Career. I remember this like it was yesterday. The cleats I chose were on the low budget end. They were a pair of thin, black and white Pony cleats. In today's society, they wouldn't stand a chance of selling against the highly favored sport brands like Nike, Under Armor, and Adidas, but to me, they were like holding treasure in my hands. I still remember exactly how they felt, how they smelled and they are still one of the most important gifts I have ever received.

Despite attending school on weekdays and working on football with Osben after school, I still managed to find time to get into trouble and it usually happened on Friday evening. I, with other kids from the neighborhood, would throw rocks into windows, vandalize property, shoplift from stores or fight. I am not proud of what I was doing, but it was just the way we kids would vent our frustrations. Osben paid close attention to my activities and decided that there was something better for me to do on Friday evenings. He wanted to stop me from hanging out with the wrong crowd and wanted to find a constructive way for me to spend my time on the weekends besides getting into trouble. Where I am from, most schools play varsity football on Friday nights. He started taking me to the Prichard Stadium to watch the Vigor High School home games. Vigor is a school where 90% of my family members are alumni, so I had a connection with the school. I could see myself one day growing up and running onto the field as a Wolf Pack player.

On Fridays, the walk home did not seem as long now that I knew Osben would be taking me to the game. I would now race home, get dressed, and be waiting when Osben came home. After freshening up we would ride to Prichard Stadium, which was only about 5 minutes away from our house. The closer we got to the stadium, the more traffic we would run into. It seemed to take forever to a young boy to get through the bumper to bumper traffic. Like us, everyone was trying to get to the game. The closer we got to the stadium, the more congested it became as people were eager to cheer their team on. I am sure it was a challenge for law enforcement to maintain order. As we would make our final turn into the parking lot in our 1995 Ford Taurus, there was always a red cloud of dirt hovering in the air, stirred up by the tire treads. As I would get out of the car and look in the air, my eyes were always greeted by the huge, bright stadium lights. We, Osben and I, usually bypassed the ticket booth and headed straight to a side gate where one of the coaches would let us in. The gate was next to the team locker room and I could hear the excitement of the players inside. Then we would hear the team recite the Lord's Prayer.

The Vigor Football Team wore hunter green uniforms that sported a white wolf logo on both sides of their helmets. The players would line up and wait on the coaches to give their final instructions before walking out of the small locker room doors. They would then begin their battle walk towards the black, rubber track that surrounded the vibrant, green playing field. As they reached the track, you could feel the adrenaline charging through their veins. It was always a special moment when they took the field, greeted by loud cheers and thunderous applause. I would follow behind the team, carrying the plastic water bottles. On some nights, if luck prevailed, I would get a chance to be a ball boy. In this capacity, I would be allowed to run the football on and off the field between possessions. When I got to be the ball boy, my face would be sore from smiling from ear to ear the whole game. I took pride in these duties and these moments meant a lot to me as a youngster. I would look into the huge crowded stands until I spotted my mom, who was always cheering loudly. She is an alumnus of Vigor High School. For some reason, I continued to hold on to the gift of being able to locate my mom in the audience, whether it was a stadium full at the Georgia Dome or the wild, roaring crowd of 85,000 in Death Valley. It never got old to me. During every game, I still become spellbound when I get the chance to experience the live action of the game.

Because of my exposure to football at an early age, I have always felt at ease around locker rooms. Football was becoming the love of my life, even though I was very young. For the first time in my life, I grabbed hold of something that I loved, outside of my family and God. With my passion for the game of football growing and my skill level on a steady increase, my dad decided to sign me up for multiple developmental and charity camps like The Phil Savage Camp in the city at Ladd Stadium. This particular camp was always structured in a competition manner. There was a fast man race at the end of camp, but I made sure I stayed away from the race because I knew I was not very fast. I excelled in the best hands competition they called the gauntlet drill. During this drill, I had to run across the field catching passes while running from side to side every 5 yards. My skills were improving and I was awarded the MVP award at camp. I felt even then that I was a rare breed with lots of potential and my small successes only increased my desire to see my dreams of playing football realized. I knew I had a future in the world of football.

Despite my father's constant efforts to keep me away from trouble and violence, I still found ways to get into trouble. For a while, my family was so concerned that my mom quit her job at Hertz Car Rental because she feared losing me to the streets at a very young age as many people in our neighborhood had. Reflecting on this now, I realized that I was making mistakes that were not good for our family. Considering our finances during this time, it was vital that she worked. The crimes I engaged in were never very severe, but I know I was a troublemaker nonetheless. Thanks to God's grace, I never got into any major trouble though, I deserved to. These times would eventually serve as learning lessons for me to be a leader, not a follower, in life. I would eventually want to take a different route and to become a person that everyone looked up to when times got hard instead of someone who people thought poorly of. I wanted to lift people's spirits and inspire them, especially kids. All through the troubles I caused my parents, my dad continued to stay on the course of developing me into being the best football player and person I could be. He felt that football was not just learned from teaching and coaching different positional skills, but also by engaging with and being around positive people. He began taking me to Senior Bowl practices or anything else that would keep me off the streets. He took me to fan day experiences on Friday and to the Senior Bowl game on Saturday. He wanted me to see the game on different levels. When we weren't doing that, we would watch games of some of the best college football players, players that would soon be playing at the top level in the NFL.

Every January the city of Mobile serves as host to the Senior Bowl game at Ladd Stadium. The Senior Bowl is a post-season all-star game, where the best NFL prospects are able to showcase their talents for NFL scouts and coaches. The teams are split into North and South rosters based on the regions where their colleges were located. This week of football was not about winning and losing a football game; it is a week for the players to have their skills analyzed by the coaches so they could decide if that player fulfilled a need on their team. They are coached by the NFL coaches whose teams finished with the worst two records. The practices were always open for fans to come see their favorite players compete. After getting approval from my mom, my dad would take me to see the teams practice each day of the week, Monday through Thursday. During that time, I would get the chance to see stars from both the North and South teams. The practice schedule was rotated daily with one team practicing in Mobile and the other 30 minutes away at nearby City of Fairhope. I would get to watch these practices and I remember going into a daze as I watched the best of the best compete against each other, drill after drill. I remember leaning on the gates, watching big throws from Ohio State's Bobby Hoying. He finished up the week winning MVP of the game.

Friday, during Senior Bowl week, was the most exciting day for me. This was fan appreciation day and was set aside for the student athletes to sign autographs. The event was held at the Mobile Convention Center, which was downtown next to the team hotel The Admiral at the time, but recently changed to Riverview. The Mobile Convention Center was the ideal spot to have this event because of its size and location in the heart of town. Fan Day always took place on Friday as the teams returned to the hotel after their mid-day walk through in preparation for the big game on Saturday. My dad made sure I got there early so we would not get caught in the downtown 5 o'clock traffic.

I still recall all of the events surrounding Fan Day. The scene inside is similar to that of huge fan tailgates that take place outside ACC or SEC stadiums when the team buses pull in. Everyone is yelling and screaming and the room was filled with excitement, passion, and anticipation. The players sat at long, wooden tables and, in front of them, were boxes filled with their first professional cards, and the players would sign them. It was easy to see where the best players were because of the long lines in front of them. Signs were hung over the tables that told you exactly who was sitting there. Through the years I recall getting autographs from players like Phillip Rivers (San Diego Chargers), Cadillac Williams (St. Louis Rams), DeMarcus Ware (Dallas Cowboys), and DeMarco Ryan (Philadelphia Eagles).

After the fan experience would end, the players were escorted back to their hotel. I would quickly follow. Most fans head home after the signings, but the love I had for football was second to none so I would sit in the elegant hotel lobby for hours waiting for players to walk through, heading to the glass elevators. I was constantly pestering them to sign something, anything. Most of the players would be tired from all of the practices that week and were eagerly heading to their rooms with family members for rest. I recall sitting in the lobby for hours until the crowd of agents, families, players, ESPN staff, NFL Network and local television stations would leave. I was always happy because most would stop because they didn't want to miss out on the time to make my day. After all, most remembered being me just a few years prior. I recall these days fondly because, later in life, I would find myself in similar situations. I would be the one the young kid would be asking for autographs. In fact, signing autographs would be something I did regularly for fans. I was always especially honored when the younger kids shared the same dream that I had as a young man. I never wanted to be the person that would turn those kids away.

After getting all the autographs I wanted, I walked back to the 50-yard field that was laid in the middle of the room for pick-up games for kids. This was really fun for me and allowed me to compare my talent with other aspiring football players. There were so many kids there. The pick-up games and drills were run by the United States Army. If any of the kids challenged me, I was eager to show off my skills and steal the show. For a heavy-set chubby kid, I would make some of the most remarkable one-handed catches and quick intensive interceptions on the defensive end. I displayed some exceptional skills for my size and the movements I displayed were extremely exceptional, especially for a kid like me whose training was limited.

Later in April of that year, I watched the NFL Draft with my dad, pick by pick, and recorded the picks in this small, black, thin notebook that my grandmother had given me to take notes in during church. This was often a long, drawn out process, but the passion I was gaining for football kept me focused. It seemed like every player that was being drafted I had met at the Senior Bowl. I was excited and it felt like I was watching a big brother get drafted. I found that I was picturing myself as one of the players, standing on the stage with the commissioner as he held out an NFL jersey. I know I am like so many other children who had this same dream, yet only a few people ever hear their names chosen. I remember watching the players, surrounded by their friends and family, looking so nervous while sitting in the green room waiting. I can vividly see the tears of joy that would begin to fall as their phones would ring. Their families would surround them and they would be hugging and kissing them. I said to myself that I wanted that same excitement and joy for my family. I wanted the satisfaction of knowing that my mom would never have to work again. I was going to do everything in my power to make sure that happened.

During the summer of 1996, at the age of 7, Osben registered me to play at the inner city Kidd Park. I was overwhelmed and excited because my dad, Osben, would end up being the coach of my team. Being on a city league team presented many new challenges. We didn't have the money for equipment, transportation, and there was no such thing as facility renovations. My mom did not have the same feelings we had about me participating in football. She was concerned about me being injured in such a physical sport. My mom would often say, "I don't want my baby to get hurt." Those words showed that she had built up a wall of protection around me, especially since she had been forced to raise me alone, in the wake of the death of my biological father. My mom would eventually buy into the whole football idea later, when she noticed how much it meant to me. She saw that it was keeping me out of trouble and was motivating me in the classroom too. Before she allowed me to play, she would contact my teacher to get a weekly grade report. If I did not meet her standards, I would not get the chance to play that week. Mom was a frequent visitor at many of the practices. And of course, she attended all of my games. She would be wearing her white sun visor, a hat or holding an umbrella to protect her from the sun. There was not a play, whether I was on the field or not, that you didn't hear her voice. I thank God every day that mom let me play.

Early in the season, she came to games bitter and angry because she noticed that my dad was not putting me in the games. I was one of the better players on the team. I just remember that I didn't understand and didn't bother to ask. I was just happy to be part of the team. One day, he threatened to take me off the team. "It is a waste of both of our time," she had said. Osben later revealed to her that he didn't think I was ready. This was the beginning of my football career. From early in life, overlooking and underestimating my abilities was a trend. What those that misjudged me didn't know is that there is no way you can measure a man's heart. Hard work plus dedication, with a little faith in God, could make miracles happen.

I guess the game that was most memorable to me was one where we played our division rivals, Peters Park. It must have been 100 degrees that day. My mom was at her usual post, standing right behind the team on the sideline. There she was, with a big, white umbrella and small washcloth so she could wipe her face. After every game, her shirt would be wringing wet because as the ball moved, she moved too. It was about the 3rd quarter on this dusty football field, which also served as the home field for the Leflore High School baseball team in the spring, and my dad was putting me in the game. My time had come. We were down by as much as 28 points and there wasn't really much at stake. The chances of making the playoffs were slim, with the second to worst record in the division. My name was finally called and the hair on my arms bristled as if I was freezing, in spite of the heat. I was nervous because I had never had the opportunity to play, except during practice. I was placed in the running back position, and I had no experience there. The play was called the huddle 28 lead and was designed for me to get the ball off to the right side with a fullback in front of me as a lead blocker. I got down into my stance and looked over to the right, just like I had been instructed, and I could see my mom. She had her cloth up to her mouth and looked almost as scared as I felt. The ball was snapped and handed to me. The weirdest thing started to happen, instead of me running forward, I began to run backwards for about 10 yards before hearing the voices of the crowd screaming, "Wrong way."

After making out what they were saying, I turned around and raced forward. By that time the other team was on our side of the field. As I ran forward, eluding would-be tacklers, I ran sideline to sideline. This had the markings of being one of the longest plays in history and should have landed a spot in the Guinness Book of World Records. Everything was going fast and in slow motion at the same time. After running side to side for about 15 yards, I found an opening on the sideline my mom was on and raced down it. This was probably the fastest I had ever run in my life because of all the adrenaline coursing through my veins. As I was approaching the end zone, I could see my mom running beside me sweating and screaming, "That's my baby! That's my baby!" In my eyes, that's when my true passion merged with hers for this violent game of football. Our life as a football family really began that day.

Sadly, the following year, Osben met a man at Shell's gas station. This guy told my dad he wanted me to come to register at their park to play that year. It seemed like a great idea at the time, though I would miss playing for my dad. So sure enough, the next season we headed to Municipal Park, 20 minutes from the house to sign up to play. This program was the total opposite from where I had come from. This park was labeled as a county league, which meant that they had better resources, fundamental coaches, equipment, support, competition, and funds. All these luxuries would be an upgrade for me. I knew that it would be a struggle for my family to find the money to drive all the way across town, especially for my mom. But to my surprise, she was happy with the prospect of my playing for a more structured organization. She made sure I had what I needed and was positive this was the best thing for me so she made it happen. That was July of 2008.

As we went to register, I was excited, nervous, and frightened all at the same time. I did not know what to expect. Osben had to work that day, so my mom took me for registration. When we made the turn into the park and through the entrance, we could see that this was a big time program. There were cars filling the parking lot and people were coming in and going out. The ages of the players determined when you registered and we had to wait a little while before it was time for me to go in. We parked as close as we could to a long building where the registration was being held. It was finally time to go in. As we signed the papers, weighed in and picked out our equipment, the coaches were checking us out. It was fun meeting my future teammates. The coach that had recruited me wanted me to play a division up because of my size but after a convincing, persuasive conversation between Coach Bo and Coach Tony Jones, Coach Bo allowed me to stay with my age group.

Two weeks later, it was time for me to head to my first practice. My mom, who is big on being on time, had me at practice at 5pm, although practice didn't start until 6. There was not a person in sight until 5:40. By that time, my Gatorade bottle had only a few sips left and I had not even run one play. It was August and I had always been taught to drink plenty of fluids to maintain a safe body temperature because of the heat. As Coach Tony and his son Phelon Jones arrived, I was relieved. Soon, as if by magic, the arrival of the coach was followed immediately by the arrival of the other players. The parents sure had everything down to a science and this was the beginning of a new world for me. Things before had always been fairly casual but not anymore.

At practices, when the loud whistle was blown, the other players and I would take off running towards the field like a herd of cattle. I could smell the grass as I entered the gates and I knew it was time for football. Each team in this league wore a uniform of a NFL team. Proudly, I was dressed in my new uniform, which was patterned after the Oakland Raiders. The helmet was coated with fresh silver paint, with a sparkle base, and a long black strip on both sides of a pirate's head. The pirate was wearing an old-fashioned, mask-less football helmet. The pirate had an eye patch over his left eye with two swords crossed in back, positioned on a black shield with Raiders written in white above him. Practice the first day was just an introduction and full of drills. Coach Parker, Coach Rod, Coach Cole, and Head Coach Tony Jones focused on fundamental techniques drill after drill and worked us hard. I felt like we were in the Marines. Practice would end with a conditioning session. Normally by this time during practice, I was struggling to cross the finish line, and at night, I would sleep hard. The following morning, I always felt as if I had been beaten with a baseball bat. I would walk gingerly, but the sore- ness just was part of the process.

I had found a football home, and for five years, I stayed at Municipal Park and played football. These five years were an important part of the development of my football career, and the place where I learned all my skills and fundamentals. We had very advanced play calling, and audible from a wristband at the age of nine. I played both Tight End and Defensive End positions while I was there. Our team surprised many other teams throughout the city with our development and chemistry. Our team was even honored by the City of Mobile for our accomplishments. We went five seasons with a record of 72 wins and only 1 loss, which took place during my first season. The title games at the end of the season were called the Youth Bowl. Our team won five title games straight. We had a great coaching staff, parents' club and they made the place and the games enjoyable, especially for a young boy from Prichard.

The games tested our faith and Tony Jones would give us a heartwarming speech after each game and practice that sounded like this: "Make sure that you guys are in church in the morning. We are champions not only on the field, but in life. Make sure you're leading the classroom. It would be a shame if we win as many games as we do and fail at life later. Be special! Lead!" Coach Tony Jones preached.

He was a remarkable man of faith, character, and dignity. He would also serve as a future father figure to me. I recall our last game; it was a cold December Saturday morning and very windy. It was our final Youth Bowl. This particular day, our team had a decision to make. We could select four members of our team to play in an All-Star Game or we could play as a team against the New Orleans All-Stars. We chose to play the New Orleans All-Stars as a team. We were a close group of guys, but this game turned out to be the wrong decision. We arrived at the stadium and were excited as we continued through our pre-game weigh-in. We met in the parking lot and we could see the stadium filled with people. Some were only there to see our team falter.

After getting dressed, Coach Jones blew a whistle that he wore around his neck to get our attention. He instructed us to form our weigh-in lines. As we started our walk towards the scale, there was the sound of click-clack as our cleats hit the floor. As we made our final turn, we were in total disbelief, because standing before us were the biggest boys we had ever played. Some of them were covered with facial hair and some even had beards. They looked to be about 20 years old and really needed their birth certificates checked. This game was lost before it even started. You could sense the fear ripple through our bodies despite the efforts of our assistant coaches who said things to try to ease our nerves.

"Let's go out with a bang! Nobody comes to our City and leaves without an L!"

They tried to lift our spirits by reminding us that we were champions and they worked. The locker room came alive. We prayed together.

As we concluded the Lord's Prayer, Coach Jones reminded us, "Last ride boys. Let's finish this thing off the right way."

United and ready to fight together for the final time, we ran out of the locker room to a roaring home crowd and headed to our sidelines. We kicked off to them and, on the opening kickoff, they sprinted down the field for a touchdown. We lost a hard fought battle by 14 points. The final score was 28-14. Two months after our loss, we learned that some birth certificates of the other team members were in fact changed, but that encouraging news did not change the results of the game we played and lost.

The days at Municipal were some of the best times of my life. I developed close relationships with guys like Phleon Jones, who now plays for the Jacksonville Jaguars; AJ McCarron, the starting quarterback for the Alabama Crimson Tide; Shaun Collins, baseball star; and many others. The final season at Municipal was the last time many of us would play together before heading to different middle schools. What remained with me and the other guys on the team were lessons, skills, work ethics, and a spiritual foundation. The values we learned would follow me all my life. I believe my meeting and playing for Coach Tony Jones was an act of God and I thank God that we bumped into each other in the store on that evening in 1996. I am grateful for the faith it produced in my mother and me. I know God made a way for me and I remember how my mother sacrificed and struggled financially for the $150 it took each year for me to participate. Even as I walked off the field at Municipal for the last time, I knew that I had already served as witness to God's favor. The Lord has a way of placing people in your life to guide you into your blessings. During this stage of my life, I had no idea that God would use my dad's introduction to a simple game of football as an avenue away from the troubles and violence that took place in my community.

The game of football is one that I had quickly grown a passion for. Through the efforts of my mom and dad, it would help me go places and reach people. I know I could not have done this without the football platform. I understood very early that this ride would not come easy and that there would be people, obstacles, and challenges that I would have to face to reach the top in this game and life. However, I knew football gave me hope and participating could keep me from being another statistic. I was up for whatever future challenges that I would have to face and with the thought "True Champions Seek New Victories" in my head, I continued my life's journey.

4

CHASING THE DREAM THROUGH HARD WORK AND DEDICATION

"And whatever you do, do it heartily, as to the Lord, and to men"

AKJ

My road to high school wasn't the clearest or most traditional route of attending one middle school and passing onto high school. My path was much more complicated and consisted of transferring to three different middle schools: Phillips Preparatory School, Scarborough Middle School, and finally graduating from nearby Hillsdale Middle School. The first of the three middle schools was Phillips. Phillips is one of those magnet schools where you had to maintain high academic marks. If you did not meet their minimum standards, you would be asked to withdraw. I started out well, but unfortunately, towards the end of the 2nd quarter, I started failing math class. I did not pass math and missed the standard, so my mom was forced to withdraw me from the school.

After Phillips, I enrolled in Scarborough Middle and finished my 6th grade year there. This move was difficult for me because it came mid-term and I didn't receive the warmest welcome from the kids at Scarborough. I was picked on and talked about every day for something different. I often wondered, was it because I was from a different area, or perhaps just because I was the new kid? Whatever the case, I did not have many friends. The following year I decided to try out for the football team. I was cut twice, but later in the season because of injuries to players on the roster, I was asked to come back out. Unfortunately, I suffered a broken ankle. My faith, which was already weak, took a direct blow.

Going into my 8th grade year, my mom met our next door neighbor, a teacher at Hillsdale Middle School. Hillsdale Middle School was located closer to our house, so our neighbor convinced my mom that it might be a better fit for me. My mom did not need much convincing because the drive to Scarborough Middle was not an easy trip to make every morning. Just trying to get me to school on time every morning was challenging because of our transportation issues, so I was transferred to Hillsdale Middle school. Our neighbor agreed to allow me to ride with her to school but unfortunately, things where even worse for me there, in terms of getting demoralized and picked on. I believed the harassment to be a rite of passage put on many of us low-key personality type of students. I eventually became immune to it. No one dared put their hands on me. I knew how to protect myself. I did not respond to the insults and harassment. I was taught "sticks and stones" and knew that words could never hurt me. My 8th grade year at Hillsdale Middle School was not all bad and I ended up trying out for the football team. The program at Hillsdale was better than each of the last two schools I had attended, and I had to work extremely hard for the little playing time that I received, but I survived and made it through the middle school carousel to my 8th grade graduation.

After attending three different middle schools and transferring twice, my parents prayed long and hard and thought deeply about what high school I should attend. In the back of my mind I can still hear the elders saying, "Young man, make sure you get that education. Nobody can ever take that from you." Personally, I wanted to go to a school that had a good football team because, at the time, that was all I really cared about.

Prior to enrolling for my freshman year of high school, I was not serious about anything except football. I was just doing enough to get by. I made sure that I was eligible to play but I never really hit the books as hard as I should have. I spent the whole summer trying to figure out which one of the three schools I wanted to attend would be chosen. The top choice was Vigor High School and it was the one with which I was the most familiar. Vigor is the place from which many of my family members graduated.

The Vigor Wolves are known in Mobile for being decked out in their green and white uniforms, and I had been a water boy and football carrier there when I was younger. They had an athletic football team, but choosing Vigor would provide some challenges for me. It meant reuniting with childhood friends which could be a distraction to my goals. Despite my attraction to Vigor, there was also the problem of distance because it was farther away from where we lived now.

My parents and I started to look more into the schools that were closer to our house. We took a long hard look at nearby Shaw High School. Shaw is where most of the students that attended Hillsdale Middle School went. I visited Shaw High School. Shaw was shaded by trees and sat back in a residential neighborhood. As I toured the campus, I loved the shade and coolness provided by the trees. I thought to myself that these trees would not be bad during those long, hot summer camps in August. The final school we visited was Baker High School. Baker is located near Mobile Regional Airport about 10 minutes from our house. Baker is known for its high academic achievement. The academics made Baker my parents' favorite, but Baker was not a football powerhouse. In fact, I could not recall anyone signing a Division-1 Football Scholarship from Baker and they were a class 6A school. I rationalized to myself this was because they had to play some of the area's toughest teams and those teams had more prospects.

It felt as if my parents and I had spent the whole summer going back and forth trying to make a decision about high school. It was extremely difficult because my parents' goal was finding a school with high academic standards and I was focused on finding a big-time football program. As we sat in our family's living area, we discussed the pros and cons of each of the three public schools. My parents continue to mention how they wanted me to go to Baker because it would be close to our home and had high academic marks. But I countered that I wanted to attend Vigor. "Vigor is where I want to go, it's my childhood dream!" I expressed emphatically. This conversation was going nowhere fast. At this point, we were simply just agreeing to disagree. After 45 minutes of deliberating we just decided to postpone the discussion for a later date. The plan to postpone was derailed a few hours later as Osben and I ventured out to get a jump on school shopping. We knew that all of the public schools in Mobile County wear basically the same uniform, which included Khaki pants and polo or collared shirts in the school colors. So we determined we would tackle Bel-Air Mall on Airport Boulevard. On that blazing hot day, as we sat in the car, we came up with a plan of how we would approach the mall crowd. I was to run in quickly for some pants because Osben expressed he did not want to be there long.

Just as we entered the mall, we ran into Clifton McNeil and his grandson Mike, who was also uniform shopping. Coach McNeil was drafted by the Cleveland Browns in 1964. After playing for a number of teams, he retired in 1973 and became the coach of his grandson's team in the Pop Warner football league. His grandson and I were on rival teams. Pop Warner Football is where my friendship with Mike had started. We face many encounters, through the heat of battle and many post game handshakes we had formed a healthy bond with one another. As usual conversations between Coach McNeil and Osben were often long and drawn out and this time would be no different. For some reason when those two got to talking, minutes would turn into hours as the conversations seemed to make Osben forget the parameters he set for the mall outing. Mike and I knew from past experience what to expect, so we searched for the nearest seats to wait patiently. I now know that this particular encounter between Osben and Coach McNeil was life-changing for me. It was no accident and God was again guiding my life.

As we were sitting in the hallway near Dillard's, I overheard Coach McNeil ask Osben, "So where is Brandon going to high school?" Osben began to answer, "Coach, we have been trying to find the best one for him to excel both in the classroom and on the football field, but we just cannot seem to find the right fit. If it's not one thing, it is another," He stated while shaking his head and smiling. "It's just not lining up, Coach." Mike and I got up thinking the conversation was winding down, but instead it took a surprising turn.

"You guys should look into Davidson, that's where Michael is heading. They also have a good football program," said Coach McNeil. Considering the bond that Mike and I had built, Davidson would be ideal. Osben got quiet then pondered loudly in what seemed to be an A-ha moment "Davidson... Davidson! How did we miss checking into that school?" He asked, as he looked toward me as if I had an answer. "It didn't cross my mind, and I have not really heard much about them," I said dryly adding my input. The truth was I understood how we could have missed Davidson, especially since we were not from the West Mobile area where there were several quality schools to choose from.

Osben thanked Coach for the great recommendation and promised to run it by my mother when we got home. As we were leaving he turned to Mike shaking his hand saying "Nice seeing you young man. There is a huge possibility you and Brandon will be team-mates." The ride home was filled with anticipation as it seemed that my new school was nearly cemented. After consulting with my mom it was settled, I was going to attend Davidson High School.

The decision for me to attend Davidson High School was made im-mediately after returning home and consulting with my mom. I was going to attend Davidson High School. Davidson encompassed everything my parents and I wanted. It had both academic and football programs at all levels, but the one low point was that Da-vidson had not traditionally been a great football team but all that was forecasted to change with senior twin Linebackers, Jordan and Dusty Lindsey, leading the team. Jordan and Dusty were prospects who signed with the University of South Carolina Gamecocks. The previous season, the Varsity Football Team finished with a 10-2 re-cord. The Varsity repeat with a 10-2 record this season but failed to reach the 6A State Championship due to losing to Vigor in the second round of the playoffs. The highlight of the season was the recruitment of the Lindsey twins.

The next year Gabe McKenzie signed with Auburn University and it started a trend. Davidson almost instantly became a college re-cruiting hot spot. I saw a variety of college, junior college, and pro-fessional coaches enter and leave out of the Davidson High School Field House. As a freshman, I found this exciting. I was motivated whenever I would walk into the Field House, I would constantly run into and be greeted notable coaches that had impacted me like Nick Saban, Lou Holtz, and Tommy Tuberville. This trend continued throughout my high school career and was as normal as practices. I saw coaches so often I felt that we were close friends. "Wow!" was the only thought in my head. Because of all of the attention from recruiters, I believed Davidson's football program to be legitimate contender and the best place for me to hone my skills.

"Brandon Maye!" This is what I heard coming from the front of the room, as I sat in the back. I was sitting on a black, dusty, powerlifting mat in the Davidson locker room/weight room area. As I heard my name, I quickly rose to my feet. I remember being a little fellow, chubby in size and weak in strength, surrounded by a massive group of freshman football team hopefuls. I responded nervously, "Here sir." It was the voice of Glen Vickery, the Varsity Head Coach at Davidson High School. He was calling roll in our first freshman team meeting. I remember it like it was yesterday. When I went to sit back down, there were crackles of low laughter coming from within the group. I was not sure what they were actually laughing at, and I wondered if I had a 'KICK ME' sign on my back. I knew that I was again the new face on the block and they did not know me from Adam. I did not know any of the guys in the room nor did I attend middle school with any of them. I took my seat and wiped the sweat off my face, baffled. I remember the end of Coach Vickery's long speech clearly. He said, "I hope your time here is one of the most memorable times of your life."

My freshman year, I had no foreshadowing of the various obstacles, trials, and emotions that I would have to endure for the next four years of high school, but I looked forward to being a student-athlete at Davidson. A few days after the initial meeting, we were divided into teams and split up for tryouts. Coach Smith was over the freshmen team. The tryouts for freshmen were held on the grassy section of the school's baseball diamond. The area was fenced in with a low cut gate. The limited space made it difficult for the coaches to evaluate quarterbacks and wide receivers due to the inability to see deep passes. Each receiver usually ended up limping back from any deep balls thrown because they typically flipped over the fence trying to retrieve them. I worked with the defensive line group. Our position coach was big on hitting the sled. Throughout the tryouts I grew frustrated continually questioning myself about the logic of hitting dummies that weren't going to hit us back.

I was pleased with the intensity of the tryouts, but sometimes I was too distracted by my attire. We wore black glitter-filled helmets, gold team shorts with the words Davidson High School embroidered on the bottom left corner, and a black jersey with white numbers. Football is typically played in a lot of protective gear so it did not make a whole lot of sense to me how someone could accurately judge your football ability when you are just wearing shorts. After three grueling days of tryouts, I was informed that I had made the cut. I competed against some very talented players that I believed to be the best in Mobile and I stood out among them, this gave me a great sense of pride.

Making the cut was extremely encouraging for me because I had not been recruited by the coaches in the area to play at Davidson. I thought the odds were stacked against me because I was unknown. I had very limited exposure in middle school, and no one in Mobile knew of my abilities. But I passed the tests at Davidson, or so I thought. I remember a time during one of the last of the practices where our conditioning was tested. I had to run twenty grassers. I believed in my heart that no matter what test they put before me, I was going to make this team. As I ran from side to side gasping for air, I remember thinking, "I can do this!"

I was motivated because I did not want to be humiliated or laughed at by my peers. The feeling of worthlessness that came from being mocked provided the fuel for the inner strength and the drive to push pass the fear of failure. I was slow in speed and weak in the weight room. As a freshman, I was often picked on by the upperclassmen and the varsity level players. Every day I was insulted. I would usually ignore them, saying to myself, *"Forgive them Lord for they know not what they do."*

I drew strength from the image of Christ on the cross, and I would reflect on how he dealt with the insults of unbelievers. There were many days that I did not want to return to practice and times I wanted to quit the team altogether, but I could not act on these feelings. There was something inside of me that made me press on. I knew quitting would give those who insulted me more to talk about and I wanted deeply to prove them wrong. I finished those grassers with confidence and I did not falter.

After practice, we headed to the showers as instructed. We were also told to hang around in the locker room and wait for the posting of the team list. I was a little nervous, but satisfied with my efforts. It took about ten minutes, but it seemed a lot longer. Then, there was the voice of one of the assistant coaches stating loudly that the list was up. Some of the guys were confident and knew they made the cut. They were probably recruited to attend Davidson and had no worries. Some of the guys showed no emotion as they dressed and began to pack their bags. I was like the latter. I did not want to let anyone know what I was feeling. I did not want to show how much making the team meant or how crushed I would be if I did not make it. I resolved to be content whatever the circumstances, but my heart was all over the place.

As I got up with my things and went toward the glass window-pane that covered Coach Smith's office door, I was both excited and nervous. Scanning the list, I saw the names... George Jordan, Calvin Rogers. A melancholy feeling came over me as I continued to scan the list. Finally, near the bottom of the list, I found my name, *Brandon Maye*. Words cannot express the mixed emotions I felt. I realized that if I had quit when things were challenging during those hot practices and humiliating weight room days, I would not have made the team. I sprinted home that day to share the good news with my mom and Osben. I found my mom sitting in the drive-way in our purple minivan that often drew attention and laughter from my classmates. She knew I could do it, and I relished in the moment.

The season started the following week. We opened our season with a loss to Murphy High School. This loss would not be the team's last. Due to our team's lack of depth, Coach Smith placed me into the position of defensive tackle. I hoped that the move was because of what he thought of me as a player, but it was out of necessity. I did not start a game during my freshman season and was played sparingly. The lack of playing time and a losing season was depressing. I believed in my heart that I was one of the better players and I knew I was one of the hardest workers. Despite my personal feelings, I chose to support my coach's decision. Being a part of a team means not letting pride get in the way of progress even if I felt I deserved to play more. I respected and understood that I was a player and the coach was the Coach. Whatever decision made by the coach, good or bad, is what he believed to be in the best interest of the team. I was a team player. I chalked it up to coaches being human. I reasoned that coaches frequently messed up when judging talent because they had so much on their minds. I took the high road and used the experience as motivation to work harder for the next season. I focused on the positive and began to develop friendships with my teammates.

Mike McNeil and I became the best of friends during this first trying season. By his appearance, one might think that he was the water boy. Mike was only about 5'7" and 135 pounds soaking wet. Mike had no muscles and was very small for a football player. What impressed me most about Mike was that it never bothered him. When he put on those pads, he came with force and intensity. Mike was a relentless, hard hitter and he let the opponents have it on the field. I noticed his hitting ability at practice our first day with pads.

I watched Mike run up from his corner back position and demolish a 6'2" running back Calvin Rodgers from Booker T. Middle School on a toss play causing a scuffle. Often at practices and sometimes during and after games, the guys would fight among themselves. The problem was lack of team chemistry there was no team unity. Getting everybody on one heartbeat was a struggle because competition was always high between the players. We were all so busy vying for playing time that practices became non-productive and when you add the fact that we were playing amidst some of the hottest temperatures humans could possibly endure you can understand why tempers flared constantly. The humidity in Mobile produces some of the worst playing conditions and there is little or no wind most days. The climate throughout the season was not conducive to winning. Instead of us coming together and becoming one, we fought against each other.

A wise man said that you are stronger as a whole, but as individuals you shatter. Falling apart was what happened to us. We fell apart game after game. My freshman year is a year I wanted to forget. Not only did we not win on the football field, but I failed a math class again and had to attend summer school. But, going gave me a second chance to pass the mathematics class and keep my grades up enough to continue playing the game I loved. The only drawback was that summer school cost money and my parents had to pay a fee for me to take the class. I was not alone in summer school. I saw familiar faces all over the classroom. I was curious and wondered why I was in a room full of class clowns. I knew I could do better than this. I passed the summer school class easily.

The brightest part of my first season at Davidson High School was developing a relationship and bond with Varsity Head Coach Glenn Vickery. He was a solid coach and was quickly becoming a spiritual mentor. He was an inspiration on and off the football field to me and other students at school, not just football players. One of his many questions asked of me repeatedly over the years was, "Who is your favorite coach?"

His influence was invaluable to me and many other students who came from single parent households, childhood violence, or those simply needing his encouragement. I can recall many days when I was down on myself or my circumstances, and a single word from Coach Vickery would turn it around.

He would walk up to me in the hall and say, "Maye, how are you today?"

With my head down, I would try hard to avoid or to dodge him. I would move quickly trying to get to my classroom before he could catch me. Those efforts would fail as Coach Vickery made it his business to make sure I was okay. I believe he sensed problems and wanted to help. He was sincere and fast. He would catch me in passing and I would have to spill it. If Coach sensed any avoidance on my part he would just meet me at my next class. It was the same routine at the entrance to my classroom; I remember asking often, "Hey Coach, How are you doing this morning?" and him replying "I am doing well, and yourself?"

Most of the time I wanted the teacher to order me inside to get ready for class, but when the teachers would see me having a conversation with Coach Vickery, my avoidance techniques would fail. Coach Vickery would tell the teacher that he wanted to speak with me outside the classroom for a minute, and that would be that. As sweat ran down my forehead and my steps came to a halt, I remember those days outside of Mr. Stallworth's Social Studies Class. "Son, what is wrong today?" Coach Vickery would ask in his deep, do not lie to me voice.

My response was always, "nothing, Coach," and I would pretend like I did not know what he was talking about. Coach Vickery knew that I had adjustment issues. He would say to me, "Brandon, you have to understand that with any change, adjustments will come."

He told me that no matter what happened in my school and football career to never let anyone tell me what I can and cannot do. He encouraged me to beat the odds. He continued by saying, "There are going to be people that doubt you and say you can't do something, but you use it and channel those words to capture greatness."

These were the only words that he would share before walking away. As I went to enter my classroom, he would look back at me and ask, "Who is your favorite coach?" I quickly replied, "Glenn Vickery." That was the truth. The talks we had in the hallways meant so much to me. I had never received discipline this way outside of my household before, so I welcomed it. My life had been a series of people passing in and out, telling me what I could not achieve and constantly reminding me of my limitations. Coach Vickery's conversations prepared me to deal with trials that I would face later in life. It was what I needed, and always at the most appropriate times. I was saddened yet happy for Coach Vickery when he took a job at Daphne High School in Daphne, Alabama. He was a great mentor for me my first year of high school and I would miss him greatly.

The words Coach Vickery shared with me in those hallway meetings would serve as motivation and inspiration going into my sophomore year. I was prepared to do something special.

I thought that, with a year under my belt, and a little more experience, things could only get better for me. The principal of Davidson High School, Mr. Copeland, hired our new Head Football Coach Fred Riley to replace Coach Vickery. I did not know anything about him, but I later learned that he was from West Alabama College and favored the option game. This knowledge created a buzz for the great backs we had on our team, Corey Patterson and LeMarcus Foney. After meeting Coach Riley, I decided to give him the benefit of the doubt. I really did not have much of a choice but to fall in line, come to know him as a person and as my new football coach. He made his presence known during our summer workouts. These summer workouts were very intense and included fast pace warm-ups. The warm-ups for the defense usually were run by Coach Session, while Coach Riley supervised.

The part of the summer workouts I dreaded most was the track because that meant we were running forty-yard sprints for time in the hot Alabama sun. As I mentioned earlier, my father was the track star, not me. I was not blessed with speed and I knew running was not one of my strengths. In fact, when my name was called, I began to sweat profusely and I would melt into a pond of perspiration because my nerves would get the best of me. Coach Riley was standing at the finish line with his pen and pad waiting to record times. "Maye," he yelled. Some of my teammates had already let him know that I was as slow as a turtle. I tried to focus and not let their adverse remarks get to me as I prepared to sprint.

"The Lord did not give me a spirit of fear, but one of power," I said to myself as I concentrated and ran as hard as I could.

My time was 5.4 seconds, which, of course, produced laughs from my teammates. I put up with the laughter because I agreed with them that watching me run was like cooking a bunch of collard greens. It took forever and a day. When I got through the finish line, I turned to Coach Riley and asked what my time was. Coach simply grinned and I remember those looks to this day. The disrespect, joking and insults often carried over to the next day. After a poor practice or performance, there was always more verbal abuse. I normally would try to shrug it off, but honestly, the remarks hurt me. This was my coach and my teammates and they were cruel. The only thing that saved me from snapping was a speech that my grandma gave me during childhood. She would say, "No matter what people say to you; the only time you need to defend yourself is if they put a hand on you." No one touched me, thank God!

As the summer came to an end, there were changes. We had a new head football coach in Coach Riley, and a new system. There were also changes in me. My body had started to change. I went from being a chunky, fat-faced kid to a skinny one with no muscles, but I made the team and practiced with the Varsity at Davidson. If you made the cut, you did not have to try out again the next season. Initially, I thought this was a good thing, but the reality was anything but. I knew immediately that this was one of those adjustments that Coach Vickery had warned me about. The speed and strength of the varsity level players was noticeable. Most days, I felt like a practice dummy. A typical practice with the Varsity Team meant being beat down for practice purposes by more experienced players until there was a Junior Varsity Game. Junior Varsity games were normally played on Thursday nights, while the Varsity played on Friday. The varsity team completed padded practices by Thursday.

My job on the team was similar to being on a practice squad in the NFL. The other young players and I were not very important, or so we thought. We didn't count in the big picture the way we saw it. The scrimmage games were used just for the coaches to see future prospects. There were some of us that played on the Junior Varsity Team on Thursday but were also allowed to play on special teams on Friday with the Varsity. I was one of those players. Playing on special teams was an easy thing to do, and I was happy that one of the privileges of playing with them was it allowed me to travel with the Varsity team to away games. This was something new for me and it made me proud to be a part of it, even if it was a small part.

My sophomore season I played tight end with Gabriel McKenzie, who later signed with Auburn University. The tight end position presented me with a note-worthy experience. Because I am normally a defense-oriented player, playing tight end allowed me to see the game from the perspective of an offensive player. I applied the lessons learned and made adjustments on the field, and in my life. It was then I really learned that we are all on a journey. Sometimes we concentrate solely on what we desire or see only one perspective of a particular situation, but in doing that, we miss so much. When we narrow our perspective, we miss out on what God really has for us. Having an open mind and learning to think like an offensive player was great. Unfortunately, I was overlooked. I did not receive much attention from the coaches and was rotated in sparingly, depending on the score board.

Wounded on the inside, I started to question myself and my ability. I wondered if I was a bad player. My plan was to beg until I got to play. It was my intention to be the "squeaky wheel" and get some grease. If the coaches were not going to play me much, then I was going to plead and bug them to death. I was going to stay after them until they gave me a chance to prove how valuable I was to the team. If the opportunity was not going to come to me, I was going to go to it. I started showing up in Coach Riley's office during lunch breaks, two or three times a week. "Coach, what do I have to do to play here?" I asked.

This blank, pale look always came over his face and he never could provide an answer. I wouldn't be surprised if he was getting frustrated with me coming every day to his office, trying to find a way to get a chance to prove myself. I think I visited his office more than his wife, who actually came in quite often. But that was not all I did.

I started coming in earlier during this time and working out by myself. I thought maybe this would get his attention. I would get on the closest weightlifting rack to his office to make sure that he saw me. I was begging him about attending camps. I worked so long throughout the season that eventually, I switched my focus to Coach Session, the defensive coordinator. Maybe he would see all the extra work I was putting in. He would see my dedication and give me a shot for some real playing time.

"What time do you guys have your game planning meetings in the morning? I want to sit in on it," I asked. I had had enough of just being a name on the roster. I wanted to contribute my talents to the team in a more significant way. I wanted to make sure the time my mom spent on Friday nights was not wasted. Instead of coming to see other people's kids, I wanted her to see her own child, shining under the bright lights on that field.

Coach Session responded, "B, we meet about 8 am, but you cannot be in the coach's meeting."

I understood, but stuck to my plan. Finally, one day as I was leaving the locker room, I finally caught Coach Session alone. This was the day my mindset changed forever. I would not take no for an answer anymore. I had just finished getting dressed in the weight room and was walking towards the two black double doors when I got my shot. I had been waiting for this moment forever. This was my chance. I opened the doors and there he was, standing with his shades on the top of his hat, tobacco packed in one side of his mouth, as he turned his coaching whistle in a circular motion and watched it wrap around his index finger. The excitement built up inside me as I drew near him. He was finishing up a conversation with another player.

I started thinking to myself, "how do I deliver this? What will his response be?"

As I made my final steps towards him, he turned and noticed me. As we made eye contact, a spirit of bold faith came over me and peace fell upon my mind. "B. Maye!" he shouted, "what can I do for you?" he asked. I confidently replied, "Coach, I am going to start here at the LB position one day!" I knew that what I said was not reasonable. I was still clocking 5.4 in the 40 yard dash.

He looked at me with a blank, surprised stare and a bold smile came on his face as he replied, "Son I respect your courage, but you will never play here, much less start for me!"

This was the quickest, most degrading conversation that I had ever had. I smiled and started to walk towards the area where my mom picked me up, trying not to let him see the devastation on my face. This conversation was one of the most defining of my whole career, both football wise and academically. It would spark a fire within me to improve all areas of my life. I even focused on playing the drums at church better. How dare he look me in my eyes and tell me that I cannot do something by telling me that I would never achieve my goal! After getting in the car, I told my mom what had just happened. I had a chip on my shoulder now and found myself ready to take my game to another level. I would do whatever it took, even if it meant me training all day.

This is when God favored me. Enough was enough. I told my mom I wanted to hire a personal trainer to assist me so I could get my speed down and get stronger. I was going to-elevate my game just to prove them all wrong. Personal trainers are expensive and not very effective, or so I learned from an advertisement warning, so I decided to give it to God. I prayed about the situation and asked God to guide my footsteps, despite what my present circumstances were. One day, he answered my prayer because Encore Rehabilitation Center came to mind. This company is known for rehabbing high school athletes, allowing them to get back to playing their sport.

Unfortunately, I spent more time there than on the field sometimes. I was a frequent visitor there. I recalled some athletes working out in the back the last time I was there. I did not pay attention to them at that time, but wondered now what they were doing. My mom and I decided to go there to check things out. There was a performance training gym in the back and the workouts were coached by Jason Poeth. Jason coached at LSU under Gayle Hatch. Jason was a short, white guy with spiky hair that stood up every time you were not maximizing your workouts. This guy had vast knowledge for the game of football, but he also knew how to prepare the mind, body, and soul. The cost for the training was $150 a month. This was not a bad investment because the reward could be greater, but it would be a challenge for me and my family to come up with those kinds of funds. In spite of that, we decided that I should enroll and I started working out there two days after registration day, which was about two weeks after my initial visit. JV football had just ended their season, and the varsity team was in the playoffs.

My training regimen became very strict. With a commitment to eating the right foods, I started on a heavy protein diet that consisted of blackened fish and baked chicken daily. The training was ridiculous. I would train with the team and, instead of playing Madden or hanging out with other kids, I would head to Encore to get my grind on. I was careful to do what was required and more. There are some people that say they want something, but then they are not willing to do the extra things to achieve what they say they want.

Well, I was not going to do that. Every workout started with a very intense warm up and stretching session. After warming up, we would always head to the platform area. The walls of this area were covered with posters of quotes from some of the world's greatest athletes: Muhammad Ali, Ray Lewis and so on. Since Jason was an LSU guy, they had a spot on the wall displaying a poster of their recently won National Championship. These posters were an excellent encouragement for me. I vowed then that, one day, Jason would have a poster of me on his wall.

Encore had a power lifting area, which is where all explosive lifts were done. I would do anything that was considered explosive to bring my time down from the 5.4 to the 4.0 second range. Jason believed that these Olympic style lifts like power cleans, hang cleans, abs, stretches, jerks, and dead lifts would create base strength in the lower body that would be converted to speed and power. Curls and bench body workouts were never a big part of the training, yet we found time to make sure we kept the guns shaped for the hunnies at the beach. I was training both at school and with Jason. I watched what I ate and, after a few months, I started to notice a difference in my body. I began to feel looser and I felt I could run faster. The training was not easy, and there were many days when it felt like my body could go no more, but I knew what I wanted to achieve and I pressed my way through. After about a month, I was beginning to feel very encouraged.

"Yeah!" Jason shouted as I walked into the gym. By the tone of his greeting I knew that the workout was going to be a significant, soul testing day and I was ready. I just smiled and said, "Let's go."

He informed me that today I was testing. I would be running the 40 yard dash today for the first time since my initial evaluation, where I was clocked at 5.4. I usually get nervous when I hear the number 40 in the same sentence as running, but today I was excited and pumped up.

I breezed through my normal workouts, wanting to build up a sweat. Today would be the day. I could see Jason setting up the lasers, which are a more efficient way to time the 40 yard dash. Jason would use lasers instead of the traditional hand-held stop watch for a more accurate time. When he was finished setting up the area, he took his post. With clipboard and pen in hand he got ready to record my time. I jogged from the middle of the indoor track, dropped my head and put my fingers on the white starting tape. My heart felt as if it was about to come out of my chest. I looked up. As I got in my running stance preparing to take off, I took a deep breath. I could feel the air pressing against my face for the first few strides and I knew it was about to be a personal best for me. I sprinted through the finish line and quickly came to a complete stop. As I turned and looked at Jason, he was laughing and smiling with joy. In two months I had dropped my 40 yard dash time. I had run it in 4.95 seconds.

The encouragement wouldn't stop there. At the bench area, I recorded hitting 20 reps of 185 pounds. This was the weight required when you went to college football camps. This feat was amazing to me, since the first day, I had barely been able to post 10 repetitions. As my body began to change, my teammates did not know what to think. Guys began accusing me of using steroids, a rumor that spread rapidly throughout the school. I was troubled by the lack of knowledge or appreciation of all of my hard work. I was putting in a lot of long, tough hours of challenging work, dedicating my mind, body and soul.

Despite their stupidity, I was being transformed into greatness. Changing on the outside gave me peace on the inside. I knew I was serving and trusting God in this endeavor. I remained humble and continued praying to God each night for an opportunity to prove myself. My faith and confidence was building right before everyone's eyes. All they could focus on was my outer appearance, yet I was learning to focus on pleasing God and submitting my natural body over to him, so that he could do a supernatural work within me.

5

GOD'S PLAN PREVAILS

"Trust in the Lord with all your heart and lean not on your own understanding; in all your ways submit to him, and he will make your path straight."

NIV

L ike any other senior football player that got playing time, the next stage was the recruiting process, which was huge in Mobile this year with players like Nick Fairley (Auburn), Ryan Williams (Auburn), Rodney Hudson (Alabama), Brandon Gibson (Alabama), and Phleon Jones (LSU). I thought with the numbers I had put up, my size, and speed that getting scholarship offers would not be a problem. I really do not know why I felt so sure of myself. I have always found myself in the position of the underdog and had odds to overcome. My process wouldn't be one of glamour. It is one filled with heartbreak and pain, which ended with a well-deserved blessing. The process that I would endure reminds me of the search for that precious jewel, for when initially found it is in a rough state, but with time, patience and hard work, it eventually becomes a diamond.

It was the week before the All-Star game in Louisiana. Around noon, we had a lunch break. This is the time that most players are out of the field house and the head coach has a conference meeting with college recruiters to go through players' records. During my high school days, this time had become my favorite part of the day and I would usually rush to the café to eat. For some reason on this day, a voice kept telling me to go to the field house and hangout. Reflecting on it now, I know it was the voice of God speaking to me. I could not grasp it at the time and even questioned whether I should go. Unbeknownst to me there was word waiting for me about my future. Not sure what I would find when I got there, I decided that if a coach spotted me I would pretend to be getting a class project from my football locker. With a plan intact, I started to walk towards the field house. As I put my hand on the door to open it, from outside I overheard two voices deep in conversation. As I continued my walk towards the locker room trying to avoid being seen, I slowly poked my head around the PowerAde machine that sat in front of my coach's office trying my hardest to see if I could see which coach it was. As I pulled my head back quickly I said to myself, "Is that who I think it is?"

In front of my coach's desk, I saw one of the finest college football coaches in the country with one of his assistants sitting there. I walked into the locker room. To buy time, I moved very slowly so I could eavesdrop on their conversation. This was easy since they spoke loudly and the building was empty. I sat on the floor of the locker room for about 10 minutes, but I was drawn to my feet as I heard my name. "Alright coaches, last player. Give me your take on Maye," my head coach questioned.

The large facility grew completely silent as the coaches thought of the best reply.

"Well...Well... Coach, we are incredibly impressed with him and his transformation to becoming a solid player." My eyes grew large, almost popping out of my head. This information was great considering the mouth it was coming from, but my smile quickly got turned upside down when I heard, "But, Coach, we do not think he can be a Division 1 player and we are going to opt to pass on him. He can really be a force on the Division 2 level and I think those are the schools you guys should inform him to target." Then they continued to rave over other players on the roster that they planned to offer scholarships to. I stood in disbelief as their words sank in. I slowly walked past the office and dropped my book bag on purpose to create a loud noise, which, of course caused all three heads to turn around. All of them were now looking at me and, I really did not care. It was as if they had seen a ghost because they all were aware that I had heard everything they had said.

As I look back on it now, I believe this conversation played a pivotal role in my future success.

I knew and understood that if this was to be, I had to create it myself. I decided my hard work was going to help set me apart from my teammates. Since field house opened early before the school day started I committed to arriving early to study film. I began to realize college recruiting was about exposure.

Many great players go unnoticed because they didn't aggressively promote themselves. I decided to take matters into my own hands devising a secret scheme to create a buzz around my name. Since most players are rated off of film and simple word of mouth, I would just help the process along. I had the mindset of a modern day thief. I would sneak into the film room, get game tapes, make copies and build my own highlight tapes. The only downside was finding a way to get the film back in the field house by the next morning. I know that my way was unorthodox, but I felt it was my only hope. Highly recruited athletes do not have to resort to these drastic measures to get noticed, but I was not in their shoes. I simply did not trust coaches anymore, and my family and I had been through and had sacrificed too much to simply leave my fate in someone else's hands. I wanted to make sure that I was getting film in front of the best college coaches in the country. I know now that I created my own opportunities by my actions. Nothing was given to me; I had to work for it. I would get with my mom and dad every night and pull my highlights from the game film. The day before I left for the all-star game in Louisiana, my mom drove to the post office and sent film to all the SEC schools, specifically to Alabama and Auburn, and to the two ACC schools that I was most interested in. I did not even consider sending my tapes to any Division 2 schools.

The next day I went to Shreveport, Louisiana for the All-Star game. I knew that this was another opportunity for me to show the college coaches why I was worthy of a better look. This All-Star game was unusual, because if you were not a top player or invited to participate in the first wave, you had to pay a fee to play. My mom did not mind paying the fee because the money was not as important as the need of exposure. Perhaps my big break would come through another player that saw me play. I approached the All-star week very businesslike during practices but made sure I enjoyed myself around the hotel and the weeks' festivities. There were some great players like Marquis Maze (Alabama Signee), Lee Ziemba (Auburn Signee), Terrell McClain (South Florida signee), and Alfred McCullough (Alabama signee) that were participating, but because this particular All-Star event was only in its first couple years, it was not as enjoyable of an experience.

I earned the name "Psycho" from my fellow teammates, because I would hide behind the dark visor on my helmet, and by making bone-jarring hits at practice. Three guys took notice to the effort I was giving and the plays I made during the week. Those three players were Mason Cloy, David Smith, and Wilson Norris. Each of them had already committed to play for Clemson University. Each had also started on the offensive line in the All-star game. They each, at separate times, had asked me if I had committed to play anywhere. I quickly replied, "I don't have any offers yet."

I took notice of each of their reactions, as each smiled in disbelief. We won the game in grand fashion. It wasn't long after returning home that I started to receive calls. I got calls from South Carolina, Clemson, Memphis, and Southern Mississippi. There were recruitment messages that said they had received my tape, some stated that they heard about my performance in the All-star game, while others wanted to let me know that they were putting me on their recruiting boards. The University of Southern Mississippi and Memphis were the first to make an official offer. The excitement and relief were welcome. Even though they were two smaller Division 1 schools, they had their eyes on me. I was just like many other high school players; I wanted to wait things out and see how it unfolded.

In early January, I made my first official visit to a college campus heading to the University of Southern Mississippi. It was a typical recruitment trip. I toured the campus, the football facilities, and the stadium. I enjoyed the opportunity to know and hang out with my player host. At the end of my visit Coach Butler told me how highly they thought of me and my abilities, and how much faith they had in my game. It was all great confidence booster considering all the work I had put in, but I left Southern Miss feeling uneasy, not at peace, expecting something better to come along.

Ring....Ring. "Hey! My name is Coach Cooper from the University of South Carolina. The staff feels very comfortable in your style of play and is ready to extend you a full scholarship offer," he explained. "This is great coach. I am honored and very interested," I replied.

During this time I became very excited when I would hear the word offer used in a sentence directed toward me. I cannot even describe the feelings of pure elation. The conversation continued with me setting up another official visit, this time to the University of South Carolina. The only things I knew about the University of South Carolina was that their mascot was a Gamecock, they had signed two linebackers Davidson High School, and that it was located in South

Carolina. The lack of knowledge I had about the University of South Carolina would change after I later signed with Clemson their bitter rivals.

A few days back from my trip to Southern Miss I headed to the field house to workout. As I walked into our team facilities I was quickly greeted by Coach Session. He asked me how was recruiting going, and asked if I'd gotten any calls from other schools.

"I have spoken with a few coaches and recently got a call from South Carolina," I replied, intentionally leaving out information about the talk I had with Southern Miss because he already knew about that. By this time I saw that I had earned Coach Session's respect and he was willing to do whatever it took for me to sign a scholarship.

"B, I personally think you should lock down a school," he said. Honestly, I agreed with his advice. I had spoken with him already and, in the back of my mind I knew that recruiting and scholarship offers for me had not come easy. Coach Session knew the recruiting game well. One day you could be the potential player they are seeking and, the next day they are on to the next recruit. If you are a highly sought after recruit, the process could be crazy...telephone calls, mail, visits from coaches, etc.

Coach Sessions decided to call coach Cooper to confirm my scheduled visit.

I studied Coach Session as he spoke to Coach Cooper on his cell phone. The expression on his face was not a good sign, and I could tell that everything was not alright. When he got off the phone, he turned to face me. "B. Maye, I have some bad news" he said. "What's that?" I asked with a curious face. "That was Coach Cooper, and he said the visit was off." I kept my head and handled it as sensibly as possible, although I wondered when he was planning to tell me. Here it was Wednesday, and I was scheduled to fly out to South Carolina on Thursday. That is a moment I have never forgotten. Coach Session comforted me. He thought it was best for me to commit to Southern Mississippi, and then let things play out from there. By taking this step, Coach Sessions said I would ensure that I would be playing college football at a Division 1 school next season. That sounded like a great idea to me. Coach Session then picked up his cell phone and called Coach Butler at Southern Mississippi. The conversation started quickly, and it seemed to me that he had Coach Butler on speed dial because he picked up immediately

"Hey. Coach I am standing here with Brandon Maye. He was telling me how he had enjoyed his visit, but did not commit because he wanted to take a little more time." Now on speakerphone, Coach Butler replied, "Yes... The visit went well coach. We wanted him to commit," he replied in his long, drawn-out voice. I was encouraged when I heard those words, but I was not prepared for what followed out of his mouth next. "He was number one on our board for a long time at the linebacker spot, but we had a kid come in the following week and commit. Now, we are out of scholarships for the year," Coach Butler informed us. My heart sank as I heard those words.

As I heard that, I started thinking to myself, what's next? I have no offers! I walked out of Coach Sessions office and over to the other side of the field house so that no one could see me. I was disappointed yet again. I walked outside and cried my heart out as I stood staring towards the sky. I did not know what my next move would be. I did not know if there was enough time left to get another offer. Positions all over the country were being filled quickly and I wondered if there were any other teams out there that would give me a shot. Both the University of Alabama and Auburn University had passed on me. Typically, if you got offers from the in-state institutions, especially Auburn and Alabama, their interest would spark others. This competition could contribute significantly to your recruiting success. I was left without any other commitments and feeling down.

I hurried home to let my family know. They were my strength during this time and never wavered in their faith, telling me that God was planning something much larger for me.

They were constantly encouraging me, begging me not to fret. Indeed, they assured me that God had something better for me. On a weekly basis, I had a telephone conversation with Coach Vick. He kept me informed about the Linebacker Coach, Coach David Blackwell, who was excited about me and my potential. Coach Vick heard that I was getting compared to another 2-star gem athlete that was graduating this season. That gem was All-American Linebacker Anthony Waters. I had the privilege of watching Anthony play, and I hoped that any mention of my name in the same breath as him would give me a shot at a college scholarship. I took this information to be an honor.

Three weeks before signing day, that hope became reality. It came during one of the typical conversations between Coach Vick and me.

Coach Vick said "B. Maye, we have been going back and forth with a few players that were ahead of you on the board, but unexpectedly they committed elsewhere." I wanted desperately to interrupt the conversation and cut him off to say, "No! No, Coach it was not unexpected, it was destined by the man upstairs," but I held my tongue and listened to him intently.

He said, "We would like to extend you an official offer. It will be mailed out to you in the morning." I almost dropped the phone. My hands started to shake. Whatever he said from that point on was a complete blur. I was in shock. "Coach Bowden and I will be coming in before the visit and set up everything."

The next week, my family and I welcomed Coach Bowden and Coach Vick into our home. This visit would be informative and significant. I knew nothing about Clemson. In fact, the only memory I have about Clemson centers on a debate I heard when I was about 15 years old. I had gone to visit my cousins Emmitt Smith, who attended the University of Florida, and Emory Smith, who attended Clemson University. They were going back and forth over who was better. I paid no attention during the debate then, but the memory of it came to mind as the coaches arrived at our home. Like no other home visit, it felt as if we were welcoming family. Coach Bowden appeared comfortable.

As soon as he entered our home, he immediately took off his shoes and walked around our house in his socks. Coach Vick was a little more reserved. I thought Coach Vick was modest and shy, until we got in our first defensive meeting and practice. There, you can tell he is in his element. There you could not get him to be quiet. Coach Vick knew defenses and every season his defenses are ranked high. They are always ranked in the Top 25 in the country. The more and more Coach Bowden talked, the more I was sold on Clemson being the place for me. I was convinced that it was all about football, yet I felt that he also cared about his players' success off the field. I believed that he wanted his guys to be good citizens, graduate from college, and go on to build great families.

During the home visit, he pulled out a picture of the last team he coached. It looked to be a team of about 80 guys.

Then he became quite serious for a moment. He looked to me and asked, "You have dreams of playing in the NFL, right?"

DIAMOND IN THE ROUGH · BRANDON MAYE

He pointed out three guys from the picture and told me that was how many players on that team who actually played in the NFL. His actions opened my eyes. He wanted me to understand that all high school players have dreams of going to play in the professional league, but only a few would get the opportunity.

I loved the fact that his recruiting techniques centered on truth. There are some recruiters out there that come into your house and focus on empty promises. Some actually will say that they are going to get you to the NFL. Bowden reminded me of Glen Vickery, my first high school coach. He was a very mild-mannered Christian. The visit lasted for about two hours, and an official visit was set for the next week. My mom made sure what happened with South Carolina was not going happen at Clemson. She did not want me to endure another cancellation of a visit. And of all her questions, the one in reference to the official visit was most important, and the one question she stressed the hardest. "He is a priority for us and nothing will change that," Coach Vick answered. My mom seemed satisfied with his response, and so was I. I think the commitment to Clemson was already made in my mind as I watch Coach Bowden with my family. He went around the dining area and hugged my sisters and grandma before leaving and walked out the door with a friendly smile on his face.

If Clemson University was anything like what Coach Vick and Coach Bowden presented to me and my family as they sat in our living area, there was no other college for me except Clemson.

The official visit was red carpet worthy. I chose to fly. This was the first time I had ever been on an airplane. My parents drove. As I sat in my seat on the Southwest airplane, I did not know what to expect. The only planes I could think of were those hijacked on 9/11, so I was a bit uneasy. I thought of how often my family and I had to settle for a long, boring ride on a Greyhound bus due to the high cost and financial strains a flight would place on my family. When the plane took off, I trembled with fear and prayed silently to myself. My heart raced.

As the plane made its last turn, the pilot announced, "Prepare for landing."

I had not been prepared for takeoff, so I knew I was not prepared for landing. I glanced out of the small window and saw one of the most beautiful sights my eyes have ever seen. It was the mountains, covered by some of the most colorful trees and the smoke hovered low over the top of them. If the scenery was any indication, I knew I was going to love Clemson.

After landing, my only thought was getting my feet on solid ground. I was officially there and I welcomed the floors of the Greenville-Spartanburg International Airport under my feet. It was an hour from Clemson, and this would provide time for me to gather my thoughts and emotions from my first plane ride. I was greeted by a graduate assistant coach holding a sign that read "Clemson Football." I had expected this because my mother had requested that someone be there when I got off the plane to ensure my safety. Surprisingly, the GA holding a sign drew major attention to me. By the time I got out of the door I had answered the question "Do you play for Clemson?" about five times. This attention was welcomed and encouraging to me. It also revealed that the fan base here was one of the best and most active in the country.

After landing, I had every intention of checking out the scenery as we headed to Clemson from the airport. Unfortunately, I dozed off minutes after holding a short conversation with Coach Bowden. I guess I was really tired and excited from my first plane ride. The first indication we were nearing our destination was a sign that read "Welcome to Clemson." I started to look around as we drove on to the hotel where I would be staying. Clemson was different from Mobile. At Clemson, I saw myself leaving my small city life filled with violence, crime, and shattered hope, to driving around cow pastures and golf courses. I saw farmland, and the smell of manure and fertilizer burned my nose. I figured that if this was in fact the place for me, it would require some adjustments on my part. I believed that I would have to adapt to a different lifestyle.

I remember asking, "God, what in the world have you gotten me into?"

I could not help but smile as I took it all in. The hotel was sitting on a huge golf course. What I quickly assessed was Clemson was a community of some of the most caring people I would ever meet. Every person I encountered, from the local business owners to the small dinner joints, was nice. As I checked in to my room, my inner voice said that Clemson was home, but I was not ready to surrender myself to these thoughts yet, especially after the initial impression I had of those back roads. I called my mom from the suite as I was watching Sports Center on the television and preparing for dinner at the stadium.

"Mom," I said, and I was happy to hear her voice! "Yes son," she responded and she sounded relieved that I had made it safe and sound. I took a deep breath before I finished. "I am not completely sold on Clemson and have not seen any football yet, but God's voice continues to speak to me. I honestly think this is the place for me. It's different here and is a nice change of scenery." "How can you feel this way when you have not really seen anything yet?" she asked. "It is a gut feeling I got from the ride in," I told her. Though she did not seem to share my optimism, my mom continued, "Okay, then we shall see. We are in Atlanta and should be there soon."

I had done my research on Clemson. I learned about the school's traditions, game day environment, coaches, players and everything. Instead of relaxing and sleeping, which were hard to do anyway, I spent my time trying to visualize how life in Clemson would be. I could see myself rubbing "Howard's Rock" and "Running down the hill." I had read all about how it was one of the most exciting 25 seconds in college football. This pre-game ritual runs deep. It was brought to Clemson by S.C Jones, a 1919 alumnus. This rock is rubbed by the coaches and players before every home game for good luck.

As the players enter Death Valley, a video plays on the Jumbotron that shows legendary Coach Frank Howard shouting, "If you're not going to give 110%, keep your filthy hands off my rock," and the cannon is fired. Amidst the sea of orange, players charge down the hill and the crowd goes wild. Evidently, the Hill has a great sense of humor because more than one player has lost their footing when running down the hill at an uncontrolled speed. After reading about the academic success of Clemson and the educational assistance given to encourage their players to succeed, I knew what to expect from that standpoint. Although I showed interest in the academic side of things, I wasn't too thrilled about the upcoming academic tour. I wanted to see Football, Football, and more Football.

The time finally came, and my family joined me along with the other recruits: Andre Branch, Miguel Chavis, Brandon and Byron Clear, and Kourtnei Brown. Most schools like to bring their players that were already committed and top targets in during banquet week, but Clemson had already had their banquet a week prior to our visit. Ours was a small group. We all loaded ourselves in waiting shuttle vans and headed to the stadium. The stadium was only three minutes away. Words can't express how anxious I was. The ride was short and sweet, and by the time we arrived, I had a hearty appetite. When we pulled up to the stadium, the lights were the first things that captured my eyes. It was one of the most amazing sites

I had ever seen. The hair on my arms and neck stood up and my body became flushed with excitement. I could see myself playing in this stadium as we drove up to the side of it. It was clear to me that it had to be one of the loudest stadiums on game day, due to the fact that it sat over 80,000 people.

We were greeted by our player hosts, and we entered through double glass doors on the side of a giant building, called the West End Zone, attached to the stadium. Each player had been assigned a player host that would guide us to our entertainment after we finished our tours and dinner. It was an honor to be greeted by my hosts Karvell Conner (Linebacker), Jock Makissic (Defensive Line), and Josh Miller (Linebacker). As soon as I met them, I knew I wanted to have the same type of impact during my college career. It would later be my responsibility to help reel in players like Tajh Boyd and Corrico Hawkins, and I had a hand in recruiting players like Sammy Watkins. I am still puzzled as to why I had three player hosts during my visit, but I really enjoyed the free meals and getting to know my potential future teammates. I know now the reason that Clemson signs so many top recruits is because Clemson can surely sell itself. We went to an area where the players and coaches had their team dinners. My eyes widened as I scanned the room seeing images of players like Brian Dawkins, Ty Hill, Leroy Hill, Gaines Adams, Jeff Davis and many other All-Americans lining the walls.

As we got off the elevator, we were greeted by the coaches and their wives. It was easy to see that Clemson was family oriented. Coach Rumph, the defensive linemen coach, and his wife spoke with me and my parents. After just a few minutes of talking with them, I knew that I would have a family away from home at Clemson, specifically a Mother. This dinner provided the first opportunity for me to meet Coach Blackwell, the linebacker coach. I had heard that he nearly turned the tables over to get me in the coaches recruiting meeting. I was anxious to meet him and honored that he thought so highly of me as a player and as a person. We exited the building and went out to the stands to a sitting area to chat about my decision. The stadium was lit up, the football field was nicely painted, and season highlights played on the gigantic Jumbotron.

The conversation went something like this, "Brandon... You know I want you to play for me. I believe you have the tools to really be a dominating force here for years to come. You possess those attributes that a coach cannot coach. I am not really into trying to find the highest rated player out there. I want the hardest working and toughest players. I feel you fill all those requirements and will be honored to watch you grow."

I nodded but remained silent. Having someone praise me like that was all new to me, and I did not know how to react. For so long, I felt many people had underestimated my abilities, and here was one of the top coaches in the country saying everything that I needed to hear.

I knew we did not have the money to pay my way through college, but I was leaning on God's faith to determine if it was the right place for me. I was not just in it for the fame of playing football; whatever school I chose had to be the right fit for me and my family. The thought might seem bizarre to some, but not to me. I knew that God did not bring me this far, from the tough streets of Mobile to this point in my life, to leave me. I trusted God and enjoyed the visit. Even though I did not have any other offers from any other universities, and in spite of the fact that I did not have a two star rating, I still worried if my visit to Clemson would end without signing a commitment.

After returning to the hotel, I kept replaying the scene with Coach Blackwell over and over in my head, as I lay in bed. I heard the voice of God speaking to me again. This time it was clear and precise. I was ready to commit to Clemson, but I did not alert my family. I had one thing left on my agenda; I had to see the academic support.

The next day, which was a Saturday, all the families, players, and coaches joined for breakfast. As I glanced around the table, I saw that all the players and I were half asleep from a long night with our player hosts. This day was set up for us to tour the facilities: Vickery Hall Academic Facility and the Football Facility. Vickery Hall Center was impressive, if not the best academic center in the country. The facilities were state of the art, and the technology was all up-to-date. Every wall was covered with images from the most memorable games and some of the Clemson greats. Becky Bowman, the director of Vickery, ran a tight ship and worked hard to make sure students were getting the tutors they needed and surrounding the athletes with the best support possible.

Later that day I met the man who would be my advisor, Wayne Coffman, affectionately known as Cheech. He made it known that he was a die-hard Green Bay Packers fan, and he had pictures all over his office to prove it. He let me know right away that he was responsible for the academic success of the defensive players on the football team. He was passionate about his job, and I sensed that he would go the extra mile to ensure my academic success. But as we went over academic information, I had a hard time concentrating. I believe I, along with the other recruits, were in desperate need of a break. Not only were we touring the academic facilities and sports facilities today, we were also planning to attend a basketball game later that night versus Boston College. This would be my first game experience at Clemson, and would really show me what I could expect from the Clemson fan base. Besides, the ACC is inarguably the best basketball conference in the nation and I was eager to see what a basketball game was like in Littlejohn Coliseum.

During the game, the excitement from the fans, and the atmosphere of that basketball game sealed the deal, and made my decision easy. I looked to Andy Johnson sitting beside me at the game and said, "I am ready to commit." Andy looked back at me smiling, and replied, "Tell the coaches, I am just the money," referring to his job as host. I informed the coaches just after the game. The excitement of me committing to Clemson overwhelmed my mother, and tears of joy rolled down her face. Coach Vick was ecstatic when I let him know that I was ready to become a Clemson Tiger. He quickly called Coach Blackwell and put us both on the phone. The conversation was full of excitement. I would be joining a class of four and five star recruits, which included two highly sought after four-star linebackers. I welcomed the challenge, and I was not afraid because life was all about taking chances.

My commitment led the way to an exhilarating and breathtaking atmosphere, as all six recruits committed and later signed with Clemson. The next morning was supposed to be an exit meeting where the Head Coach would make a final attempt to try to persuade the recruits to commit to the university. This particular exit meeting was different, in that we simply talked about report days, what to expect, roommates, and what to do with the paperwork on signing day.

What I learned on my official visit to Clemson was that Clemson was the spot for me, and I wanted to spend the next four years of my life there. I had high hopes, and I wanted to play as a freshman. I understood and accepted challenges. I knew I would be competing against two seniors for playing time. I also knew that I was the lowest rated player in my position, but for that moment in time, I was just excited to be a Clemson Tiger. I eagerly looked forward to my future as I boarded my flight back to Mobile.

Weeks passed after the visit, and on signing day, I was alongside my teammates sitting behind a long wooden table, inside of Davidson

High School's new auditorium, signing to play football at Clemson University. Humbled, and surrounded by my parents and local news media, with orange balloons all around and behind me, I began to replay what I endured to get to this point. Not long before, this day seemed impossible. There were people in my life who had doubted I could achieve my dream, when I walked on campus as an unorthodox freshman. This was a special day in my life.

My signing with Clemson University meant I had received a full scholarship to a Division 1 college. My hard work and dedication had finally paid off. The hours spent training with the team, followed by another training session with Jason, was about to pay big dividends. I remember how proud my mom was throughout the whole process. I think often of her smile. She really lit up the room. She made sure I was dressed in the best, and took me shopping the day before I signed. The black pin-striped suit, orange shirt, and orange patterned tie complimented my accomplishment well. I had overcome every obstacle and I was dressed to impress. Full of emotion, I signed the papers.

DIAMOND IN THE ROUGH · BRANDON MAYE

6

IDENTIFYING QUALITY

"You don't run from losses. You go through them, because when you go through them, that's what builds a man, that's what builds integrity, that's what builds character- going through things, not around them."

Ray Lewis

In July, a day is designated for the freshman signing class to report to campus at Clemson University. This day is now a distant memory to me. To be honest, I do not even remember what day of the week it was. I remember the day only because of what occurred in my life. It was during this time that I made a promise to myself to one day play in the NFL. I had already realized my dream of playing for a Division I college, and this was just another step in the process. It was an emotional day that began with family and friends gathering at our house for breakfast. My mom had prepared a buffet with grits, eggs, sausage, bacon, toast, and fruit. As I scarfed down breakfast, Mom and I had a conversation. I revealed to her my plan that I was going to attend college, get a degree, and play in the NFL. I clearly understood that football would not last forever. I knew if given the chance, there could be challenges. I chose to focus not on the "what ifs." I chose to have faith, trusting in the goodness and knowledge of God. I shared with her my dreams, and promised her that when my dreams became reality, she would never have to work again. She, in turn, made me promise her that if my plan did not work out the way in which I planned, that I would keep moving forward and be a light for our community. On this day the word 'can't' was removed from my vocabulary.

After breakfast, hugs and kisses were exchanged in the front yard as we packed my things in the trunk of the rental car. The drive to Clemson was six hours long, and we had to leave early to make the 5 pm check-in time. As we backed out of the driveway, it hit me that I was actually leaving the nest. Leaving the protection and comfort of home meant it was time for me to become a man. I had never been away from home before, but I realized that it was time to live my life and experience new things. My ultimate goal was to get an education. I was confident because of the values bestowed upon me by Mom and Grandma. As we were turning the corner, I heard a voice outside of my open window say, "Go forth and shock the world!"

It was my 80 year-old Grandma, standing in the front yard holding her walker. I left home with my dreams, values, and the encourage-ment from those who mattered most. I knew in my heart, I would be fine.

Just before getting on the highway, we made a stop at a gas station to fuel the car and get snacks for the road. Normally on long trips, I would sleep. Today, I just sat in the back of the vehicle with a towel covering my face so my parents could not see me. The six-hour drive allowed me to reflect and meditate.

I closed my eyes and mulled over the statements I had heard, "You can't do it. It's not in you. You are just like the rest of them. You are not good enough. You are not fast enough. You are not smart enough. You are not rated high enough according to recruiting services to play Division 1 Football. Perhaps you should look at Division 2."

I wondered why so many people at various stages of my life had been so negative. Did they want me to fail? I decided to think about what I could achieve and what attaining success would look like. I wrote down each and every negative statement on a sheet of paper, balled that piece of paper up, and threw it in the trash can. I chose not to defer my dreams or quit. I would use negative statements as motivation for my success. I wanted to prove them wrong.

As I rode along, I recalled an incident that involved one of my high school teachers. I was not a great student in high school, so just trying to enroll in Clemson University was an obstacle. I barely got in because an administrator advised me to just stay home my last semester of high school. His intention was for me to flunk out. He also wanted me to avoid any contact with one of my female teachers. I do not remember what the problem was, but there was a problem between us. It was obvious to me she did not care for athletes, or me.

The teacher's words to me were, "You will never make the grades to go to college. If you get lucky, you will flunk out in the first year and be back in the streets like the rest of them."

I did not understand why this teacher had a problem with me. I was insulted by her stereotype of me, yet deep inside I had to admit that, at one time in high school, her comments were valid. I had not taken full advantage of my educational opportunities. I was trying to be cool and fit in with the boys. I could have done a lot better. I could have applied myself and focused more in class instead of hoping to pass in the final hours. I sighed as I thought of how sad it would have been if I had listened and given up. As we pulled into campus, I sat up in the back seat of the car and looked out of the window. I was grateful for her admonishment. I thanked her at graduation. Her words would serve as motivation for my college classroom success. As I looked out my window, I saw a sign that read Welcome to Clemson. I knew I was home.

We arrived at Lightsey Bridge around 3 pm, an apartment complex on the campus of Clemson University. It is the place where all freshman signees lived there first year of college. It would be my new home. As I got out of the car, my family and I were greeted by Willy Korn, Jarvis Jenkins, Chad Diehl, and Xavier Dye. These guys were from South Carolina and did not have to travel as far to get to campus. They were characters. They rushed out to the car to help me gather my belongings and assisted me as I was moving into my apartment. With my parents' departure, I began to feel a little homesick. I just sat in my room organizing things with Andre Branch, as he was to be my roommate during freshman year at Clemson. He was from Richmond Virginia and played defensive end.

Our recruiting class was rated #16 in the country and consisted of twenty-three guys. I had spent most of the summer reading articles about my soon-to-be teammates. I wanted to get an idea about who they were as people, as I would be spending the next four years on the team with them. At first glance, I thought that some of these guys were grown men or the fathers of other students. They were big, muscular, and hairy. The appearance of my teammates was the last thing on my mind. There was a honk of a horn outside the door. It was Willy Korn. Willy was picking us up for our first team meeting. Many of the other players like me did not have transportation, so we caught rides with teammates, like Willy, who had their own cars. I did not know what to expect. I was a bit nervous. Willy helped calm my nerves with his great sense of humor. He was our five-star jewel of a quarterback and he was not threatened by the limelight.

This team meeting was the first time since my home visit to see Head Coach Tommy Bowden. I was anxious to see if the man he portrayed himself to be in my home was the genuine article, or a fake. I had heard rumors that Coach Bowden was a CEO type of coach that oversaw his program from a distance, and interacted with players only when necessary. He trusted his assistant coaches and allowed them to do their jobs.

We arrived at the team meeting room around 7:30. When we entered the meeting room, I noticed some of the faces in the room from watching football games on ESPN. There were players like CJ Spiller, James Davis, Aaron Kelly, Jacoby Ford, and Chris Clemons, just to name a few. I have to admit I was nearly star struck when I met CJ Spiller for the first time. Inside the room, the walls were covered with pictures of former players and photos depicting various victories. I understood the magnitude of in-state rivalry games, but I had never experienced being in one as a player. However, I enjoyed looking at the photographs of Clemson victories over South Carolina. I was also excited about Clemson being my new home. Players quickly took their seats, as Coach Bowden took the stage and stood behind a small, wooden podium organizing his notes. While Coach Bowden was speaking, I looked down at his feet. He did not have on any shoes. The funny thing is, I thought that he only did this on my home visit. I figured that he was confident and comfortable in all situations.

After about thirty minutes, I was convinced that the initial impressions I had about Coach Bowden were true. Our first team meeting went on for about an hour before they asked the entire freshman class to introduce themselves. Some of the players in the room were more comfortable than others. They had already developed friendships with some of the veterans on the team. I had never attended a game at Clemson University, and I had always struggled when it came to speaking in front of peers. Anticipating this moment, I had practiced the words I would say in front of the mirror before we left the apartment, and again in Willy's car on the way over to the meeting.

I rehearsed, "Brandon Maye, from Mobile, Alabama, linebacker."

I knew first impressions were lasting. I could not mess this simple task up. I wanted to make my voice deeper and let my teammates know I meant business. I did not want anyone to realize that I had a slight tremor in my voice. The player who went before me, Marcus Gilchrist, had done such a great job with his introduction that I felt pressure. He spoke with poise and confidence. Now it was my turn. I stood up, looked around, and said, "Brandon Maye, Mobile, Alabama." I paused for a long time before someone shouted out, "linebacker!"

The whole team burst out laughing. This was definitely not the way I wanted to start things off. I had been the target of laughter in other team meetings during my high school career. I had wanted college to be different for me. Now, I felt like that awkward, chubby-faced, insecure kid again.

The next week was tough. For the entire first week we did not train with the team. All freshmen had to wake at 6 am and report for academic meetings in Vickery Hall. The meetings were informative, yet long, and took away from our time to train with the team. Instead, we had developmental workouts after the academic meetings.

I understand now the value of those early academic meetings. Their purpose was to help the new players prioritize academics, and teach us the skills that would aid us in our pursuit of college degrees. I am grateful for what I learned in the meetings now. I learned how to work the university's computer system, how to sign up for tutoring, the academic integrity code, and so much more. Without those academic meetings, I would have been confused.

They were all the more important since I had had academic issues before. These were as pivotal for my academic success as the drills I ran on the practice fields were to football.

But then I was young and immature. I often questioned, "Did they bring us here to be scholars or to compete on the football field?"

When we actually did start training with the team, I almost wished that we had more academic meetings to attend. Practices were challenging. Head Coach Bowden and his staff were nothing to play with. The workouts were intense and tested you physically and mentally. Each day, we weight–trained prior to conditioning. We ran hills, pushed and pulled sleds, ran 100 meters, and completed 300 meter shuttle runs. I stayed in front of the pack on most of the runs to make a statement. I wanted everyone on the team to know that I was there to play.

Practices provided a great opportunity to catch the coaches' eyes. Even when coaches were out recruiting, coach Batson would report what occurred to the other coaches. Marcus Gilchrist and I would leave the rest of the freshmen at times to run on the practice fields. Marcus was disciplined and a hard worker. I was glad there was someone who seemed as interested in proving himself as I was. By the end of the summer, we were fitting for equipment and the Fall Camp was about to begin. After I finished my fitting I walked out of the equipment room and bumped into Coach Blackwell. Jokingly he said, "Are you not going to hit anybody?" referring to my helmet. I laughed and confidently responded, "I was born for this!" "Alright, we will see," he concluded.

College Football Camp was obviously different from high school. The first day of camp was the toughest. The team and staff were the only people on campus and it was all about football. We would meet all day and practice in the evenings. Two-a-days really tested one's physical shape. We were required to sign in at the café for mandatory breakfast about 8am in the morning. We were dressed and ready for practice about 9:30 am in our meeting rooms. Coach Blackwell, the linebacker coach, would add humor to the morning sessions, which made things better.

After our meeting, we headed to the field.

Our first fall practice lasted about two hours. After two hours in the scorching South Carolina sun, showers were necessary and required. Players quickly rushed in to the locker room to shower and take advantage of the few hours of downtime we would have. We would eat the mandatory lunch and get a quick nap in before returning for the evening session of practice. Sometimes we would not leave the facilities until late. I adjusted to the tough schedule and performed well on the football field. I did some things early that were unexpected. I made plays and put out an unbelievable effort. My hard work made the coaches take notice, and I rotated in with the second unit. There was a heavy battle going on the field between two senior linebackers for the starting middle linebacker spot. I had to take advantage of all my opportunities.

Working hard allowed me to start on the special teams. It did not matter to me at the time where I was playing, as long as I was in the rotation and I was not redshirting. I was fine with whatever role I had on the team. We were too busy to think about home. When the homesickness would hit me, I would call my family, but usually I kept the calls short and sweet. It was always good to hear their voices. But, I didn't want mom to worry about me, so I would just always tell her things were all right. The second team scrimmage was held in Death Valley Stadium. In this scrimmage, God revealed to me that he had a different plan for my life. Things were coming easy to me on the football field. I knew that this was my last opportunity to show my coaches that I was ready to play. I had already done some things on the football field that were not typical of a freshman.

Coach Blackwell informed me of my opportunity to work with the starting unit. He obviously thought I was ready. He said the last thing he would want to do is waste my redshirt season. I respected his honesty. Most freshmen are not physically or mentally able to come in and play their first season. There is also the added stress on you academically. Once classes start, because of the travel and missed classes, academics can become very challenging. The redshirt year is often used to allow time for making adjustments.

On the second possession of the second team scrimmage, Coach Blackwell came to me and said, "You are ready and you are going in next possession." My eyes lit up. "I am going in," I said to myself. I stood on the sideline trying to figure out what unit was on the field. I wanted desperately for this possession to be with the first offense. I have never been scared on the field, but in this moment I nearly wet my pants.

Before I went out on the field, I remembered those words that my grandma said to me before I left home to come to Clemson. "Shock the world," she had said. Her words were life and I was pumped up now. This opportunity would determine if I would be redshirting my first season, or contributing immediately to the team's success. I was relentless. I got four solo tackles and two for a loss.

When I returned to the sideline, Coach Blackwell said to me, "Son, you will be playing this season." I was excited. I was ready for it. I looked from the field as my coach called the play. It was a simple blitz designed for me to go into the C-Gap, which was something I had done a million times before. I took my position at middle linebacker, and got in my stance. I was looking out the side of my eye at the spot I was supposed to be blitzing. Cullen Harper, the quarterback at the time, started making his audible calls. I started to creep up, trying to time it up. While biting down on my mouthpiece in anticipation, the ball was snapped. My excitement turned quickly to terror. In one possession of the football scrimmage, my whole life changed.

As I pushed off with my right foot, severe pain rushed into my foot. I took two more steps and fell into the arms of offensive linemen Thomas Austin as he was setting to pass protect. I laid on the grass, facing the sky, shouting as tears slowly ran down my face. For the moment everything was distorted from the pain. My magical run, from being the last in my class to sign to getting sufficient playing time as a true freshman, was over.

The worst news was confirmed by Danny Poole, the Head Trainer. I had broken my foot. This would mean I would be out the rest of camp and for the first two games. It would mean I was sidelined for at least six weeks. I did not want to accept this news and remained optimistic about coming back and playing as a true freshman. Initially, the broken foot injury hurt me physically and mentally. Any athlete will tell you, getting hurt is like punishment in so many different respects. I was alone, secluded from my teammates.

Because of my injury, I had to go to an area on the side of the practice fields known as Muscle Beach. Muscle Beach was like the outside weight-lifting area at the State Penitentiary. Beach was a misnomer, as it was the farthest thing from one. The area was torture in the form of all kinds of training equipment. There was a bench press, kegs for different exercises, and pull and push machines. No matter what body part was injured, there was an apparatus designed to strengthen it, and your other body parts as well. The Training Staff made sure you did every repetition. I felt like a caged animal. Having to rehabilitate my broken foot while my teammates were practicing was difficult.

The time spent on Muscle Beach was like serving a prison sentence, but there was some perks. I spent a lot of time with the strength coaches and developed friendships with the staff. Not only was I doing what was necessary to get back on the field, but I had an edge when it came to developing my strength. I would be stronger and able to compete with older, smarter, more developed veteran teammates. I was really excited when the Fall Semester Classes began. Camp was over and students would now return to campus. I would experience college life. I would wake up for classes by the sound of an alarm clock instead of Momma's voice. I would eat on a training table instead of Momma's home cooking. I would move from a teaching environment to a learning environment.

My time management skills were lacking, and there was a price to pay for being late. I was late for my first three classes, which resulted in early punishment work from the coaches. Coaches do not enjoy leaving their families early in the morning to deal with player issues. Coach Blackwell made sure you did not make the same mistake twice. His disciplinary methods were harsh. He called it "Boot Camp" conditioning, and it was specifically designed to produce vomiting after. And if you crossed him again, you faced even more severe training like flipping tires, running on a treadmill (on his watch pace), and sprint work. College also meant choices. Once students returned to campus, there were distractions in the form of girls, parties, and drugs.

I was constantly reminded of Coach Bowden's words from our first team meeting, "Every action, whether good or bad, is a reflection on you, the team, the university, and most of all your family."

Because I never wanted to bring shame on my family, myself, or my teammates, I tried to avoid those distractions so I would not get into trouble. I was also too busy being focused on playing my first season to get involved. I watched and learned from the mistakes made by others. I had my share of fun too. I did not want to distance myself from my teammates. I just wanted to play as a freshman, so I did not always hang out with the guys. The opening game of the season was quickly approaching.

Many of the freshmen that were slated to redshirt changed their focus from football to enjoying the college experience, but I continued to focus on my goal to play as a freshman. I was busy making adjustments and did not have time for distractions. I had to adjust to being on my own. I had to adjust to going from one end of campus to the other for classes, and being there on time. I had to manage my own time and focused on making positive choices. My days consisted of study hall, classes, football practices, and meals, in no particular order. It was not as easy a transition as I had hoped. I was amazed at the number of students on Clemson's campus, and thankful that I was now officially one of them.

When I was alone in my room, often I thought about how this small rural city transformed into a circus on game days, hosting approximately 70-80,000 people. Although I was still nursing a broken foot, I was excited when the first game finally came. I woke up with a sense of gratitude for being alive and having the opportunity to be a Clemson Tiger football player. I was excited because I was a day closer to actually being on the field. I had never attended a live Clemson game before today. The date of the opener was September 3, 2007. I had anticipated my family traveling from Mobile and sitting on the 50-yard line watching me play, but now instead I cherished the experience of wearing my game jersey and supporting my teammates. The game was called the Bowden Bowl because of the father-son rivalry between Tommy Bowden and the legendary Bobby Bowden. It was special simply because it was Clemson vs. Florida State.

I begged my mother not to come to the game because I was still injured. "You can save that gas, mom. My mom replied, "I want to see the game up-close." I laughed knowing that she was using coming to the game as an excuse to see me. Game days were always special to me because of the sacrifice my mom and dad made to come whether I played or not. They would drive all night after work, watch the game, and almost immediately drive back home to Mobile when the game was over. Acknowledging their support and selflessness meant staying up all night, until I knew they were safe at home. During those sleepless nights I struggled, knowing that if something were to happen to them, I would blame myself for the rest of my life.

Game day for a redshirted player was typically a different experience from that of a travel guy who stayed with the team at the hotel. Despite being separated from the team, it was quite the experience from a player standpoint. I could feel the adrenaline rushing as we made that long, supportive, traditional Tiger Walk into the locker room. That day when the shuttle dropped us off, I was amazed to see all these people. It looked like a sea of orange as we passed tents with fans shouting to us, "Go Tigers."

We were dropped off at the front door of the stands. Some players would head inside to the locker room to wait on the traveling squad. But, I took this opportunity to interact with kids, tossing the football and signing autographs. I was just honored to be in the position that someone would run up to me and ask for me to sign something.

That season my family formed a very tight connection with this Christian family, the Cash family. Ms. Cash, who was like the team mom, was always consistent in her delivery of brownies throughout the week, reading all the daily papers, cutting sections out where a player was featured, putting them in a folder and delivering them to the players herself. Her husband Bert was also a spiritually grounded person with a caring, kind heart. Her son Bert displayed the same God-fearing values that his parents did. I guess the apple did not fall far from the tree. My family became a part of their tailgate. No matter what game or how many people came up with my family, the Cash family always made sure that everyone was served and fed.

As the team would head to catch the awaiting bus for the traditional ride to the "Hill," I looked at the audience and I remember thinking to myself, "Is this really happening? Do I really have this number 34 jersey, which I wore freshman year, approaching the sideline as the massive 80,000 orange faithful fans scream their lungs dry?"

At that moment of my life, nothing else mattered but that I was standing on the sidelines playing for the Clemson Tigers, a Division I school. So many times through my life, people said that it could not be done. As I stared out into the huge crowd, I began to reflect back on some of the great athletes that came from my community. I could not help but think to myself that I was not much different from them. But instead of giving into the temptations of the street, I had chosen to say to myself, "Let's go." I understood that getting a reward meant that first you had to sacrifice. At that moment, I realized that it had all been worth the wait. As I stood there looking at the 80,000 screaming fans, my whole life seemed to have meaning. I knew I was exactly where I was meant to be.

Suddenly my thoughts were interrupted by a loud "Boom!" It was the cannon, which sent the team charging down the orange carpet emblazoned with the white tiger paw in the middle. I was a freshman and had never experienced crowd noise like this. But even after playing in the ACC for 3 seasons with 80,000 screaming fans at Death Valley, or another season playing in the SEC, with fans ringing cowbells at Mississippi State, nothing could be as special as this moment.

The night games were usually the loudest because that gave fans extra time to drink, filling their system with beer. It was during night games that the crowd screamed uncontrollably. My traveling suit was gray, with an orange colored shirt with the paw imprinted on the pocket, and black traveling shoes they had given us to wear on the sidelines. The game was scheduled for 8 PM that night, prime time. Everyone had high expectations for our team that season. We had been rated in the top 25 in defense.

The game, which was being played on ESPN, was good advertising for the school. Big plays from both teams could be seen on both sides of the ball that night, from the superhero run by James Davis to the big sack by Phil Merling. We won the game 24-18. I was excited to just be a part of the team, something that was bigger than me. Since victories at this level were never easy to get, we celebrated every victory in the locker room. Then we turned the page to the next opponent.

That big win provided our team with a boost as we won the next three games over opponents Louisiana Monroe, Furman and NC State. Our first loss of the season came during our game against Georgia Tech. After walking away from the stadium that night, I knew I had work to do to play on this level. Seeing CJ Spiller from the sideline was like watching a flash of lightning. The skill of the players in that game verified what I already knew. There are no shortcuts in life. The only way you achieve something is through hard work.

It wasn't until after the game against Georgia Tech that one of my fears for my first season at Clemson became a reality that it was going to happen in the back of my mind because it was game 4. I was not going to get to play football as a true freshman. Sometimes in life, we have things planned, but little do we know that our plans may interfere with God's plan. During this time in my life, I didn't understand why or have a clue why He was doing this to me. I had worked so hard for this opportunity, this chance to beat the odds. I also wanted to show those who said I couldn't play football as a true freshman that they were wrong.

After being redshirted my freshman year, my life quickly took a turn for the worse. I became homesick and started calling home 2 to 3 times a week. I would tell my mom I wanted to come back home. She often replied in a mad voice, "Pack your stuff and tell Coach Bowden that you are quitting. You go ahead, come home and be another statistic."

My mom really knows how to motivate me. She knew that I would not quit if she told me I was just going to be another statistic. I knew I would be selling myself short if I gave up, so I just hung in there, but it wasn't easy. I had become so bitter and so angry that I could barely perform my duties on the scout team. I was mad at the world. Throughout every practice, all I thought about was game day. I really was not interested in just being a crash test dummy like so many of the other guys. I would practice with a chip on my shoulder. I think I was used to being the underdog.

I played with a violent intensity, and Coach Bowden sometimes would just make me sit on the sidelines for the remainder of practice. I wanted every player and coach to feel my pain. I knew that I was not going to get better as a player sitting on the sidelines. The only way I was going to get better was to play against great offensive players like CJ Spiller, James Davis, Michael Palmer, and Barry Richardson. Playing against that caliber of player did allow me to relieve some of my frustrations. But instead of taking it out on other opponents, I was taking it out on my teammates. While I would later become a big part of the success at Clemson University, the effort I gave on the scout team was not that important to me. Other players did notice my effort, and they started to praise me as they saw that I was gaining speed, agility and versatility. I gave them a run for their money.

On the weekends, I started partying and drinking. I was doing all the things that went against the values that I had been taught as a child. The devil was chasing me because he had seen that God was working in my life. I knew if my mother and grandmother saw me, they would be very disappointed in me. I had never been in this situation before, and I would have to search to find my own identity. While in the shelter of my family, I had been able to avoid these types of problems. Even though I grew up in a rough neighborhood, my family had always shielded me. But now, I was on my own. I became distracted from the big picture. I started to sleep in, and I did not go to class. My grades, which had never been very good to begin with, began to drop. I failed a class that semester. Though I had achieved a lot my freshman season, I had not been able to accomplish everything I had planned.

Even though I was engaged in many negative things, God still favored me. I had captured the eyes of the coaches, players, and the media. I had to make up in my mind, that if my future was to be as bright as I hoped, I was going to have to change my ways.

During one post practice interview, Coach Bowden said this about me, "That Brandon Maye is going to be a player if we can get him to harness his emotions, darn it, I have to sit him on the sideline during scout period to get practice reps. He is a disruptive player."

I knew the things that I was doing were destructive. It was not right to be partying, drinking, and not going to class. I was getting into fights with teammates and was earning a bad reputation, but nothing seemed to dampen the anger that I felt against the world. During one Monday night team meeting, Coach Bowden challenged me. He said that I needed to learn to value the chances that I had before me. Somewhere along this journey, I had forgotten about the endless pain and struggles I had endured as a child to get this far. It was at that moment that I knew I had to make a change. I had never been excited about a team meeting before that night. Team meetings were usually boring, and you had to listen to them talking for hours as you fought back sleep.

During that team meeting, we were getting ready for the upcoming game against Boston College. This was not just any ordinary game. We actually had something to lose. We were playing for the right to participate in the ACC Championship Game. Boston College was led by two great all-conference players. Their offense was run by quarterback Matt Ryan and their defense was led by linebacker Mark Herlich. Coach Bowden and his staff were desperately looking for something to give our team a boost going into the big game. As usual, he was doing his normal routine, walking shoeless on the stage in front of us. For some reason, I was nervous but I did not understand why. I was racking my brain trying to think if there was any way that Coach Bowden could call me out. I know I had given him enough of a reason to do so, that was clear. Since we were in the middle of the season, coaches rarely paid any attention to anyone on the scout team so I thought I was safe. That all changed 30 minutes into the meeting.

Coach Bowden asked, "Where is he? Where is he? Where is Brandon Maye?" Coach Bowden searched around the room, trying to locate me. He had just been talking about cobra snakes and how they raise their head to attack. He was referring to how our team needed to start in the big, upcoming game. His head went from side to side as he scanned the room looking for his target, me. Once he found me, he lowered his glasses.

He said, "There he is. Maye, stand up." By this time, my armpits were soaking wet as I stood nervously looking at my peers. I did not know what was coming.

| *From Humble Beginnings to Promising Future*

He continued, "See this young kid, he understands how to attack; I have to sit him on the sidelines most the time just to get some practice in."

He stood there on the stage with his hand up, in a position similar to that of an attacking cobra. I was excited. In this huge room of talented players, the coach was using me as an example, heading into the biggest game of the year, outside of the South Carolina/Clemson rivalry. That excitement was quickly shot down however, and I would've liked nothing more than to crawl under the chair. Then Coach Bowden turned and looked at me again, and jokingly he said, "Now on the other hand, he is going to be an even greater asset for us in the future if I can keep him off the grade report list."

The grade report list was a list you definitely did not want to be on. It was a report of players that were in danger of becoming ineligible due to academic reasons. My name being on the list was not a reflection of my ability in class, but it was because I had chosen to focus my efforts on getting in trouble, as opposed to homework. Coach Bowden's words during that meeting weighed heavily on me for the rest of the week. I came to the conclusion that I would have to do everything in my power to keep my name off that list. Football would not last forever. One single injury could ruin your football career. Having the injury earlier in the season had taught me that. With his words echoing in my mind, I decided to do a 180° turnaround. This would mean getting back to my basic values of hard work and dedication. No matter what the future held, I was not going to be deterred from my dreams. As the Scripture says, I would not be moved.

My plan was now intact, and I was ready for a change. I was going to chase greatness. I began by exceeding the 10-hour minimum we were required to be in study hall. My grades started to go up and the weirdest thing was happening. I was happy with where I was again. I started to actually enjoy class and learning something new. I started enjoying interacting with the teachers. I couldn't help but to think back at all those teachers who said this would never happen. And the best thing about it was, my name was off the list.

Becoming a success in the classroom not only helped me academically, it helped my spiritual growth as well. I had always been able to depend on my family for spiritual guidance, but now I was learning to depend on myself. My family had always been one of faith, but now I was becoming a person of faith. This was the point in my life that I decided I wanted to have a personal relationship with God. Throughout my freshman year, I had been slow to pursue that relationship. The reason for my reluctance was simple. Sadly, I was worried about what my teammates would think of me. How would it look, me, a big football player professing my faith? Would I look like a hypocrite because of how I acted earlier in the semester? The coaches at Clemson had always encouraged us to go to church and to study the word of God. That recommendation was embraced by some, but others stayed in their dorm room on Sunday mornings.

While in the locker room that season, I started to take notice of the FCA magazines that were seated in certain players' lockers. I would walk to their locker and look up to see whose they were. They included Thomas Austin, Michael Palmer, and Tyler Grisham. I stood there in front of their lockers thinking this could not be right. Thomas Austin was one of the meanest, toughest, strongest linemen on the team. Michael Palmer was not the strongest, but he always delivered huge plays on game day. Lastly, Tyler Grisham was one of our star receivers that just seemed to make plays every game and did all the little things right. Knowing they were able to profess their faith openly removed all fear that I had of what others would think. Knowing that some of the toughest players on our team had the FCA book in their lockers increased my faith. This was huge for a young freshman that was trying to find himself spiritually.

Not only were these players great on the field, they were excellent role models off the field too, especially for a young man like myself that was just starting his spiritual journey. They were after a much greater reward than a win; they were looking to hear those words, "Well done, my good and faithful servant."

From that moment on, I was sold. I wanted to follow their lead. They informed me that they held a weekly Bible study at the home of Will Huss, a local business owner, every Wednesday. Those meetings were some of the greatest times of my life. Throughout every meeting, I knew things would only get tougher because I had changed teams. I was now a Christian, and the devil would fight me every step of the way. The supportive members of my group help solidify my faith. That faith allowed me to escape the world of football, and to rest my mind on his word. It was the relationship I had longed for. It was the relationship that I needed.

I had already become a member of the spiritual mentor program that the team chaplain, Tony Eubanks, had established, but I had never really focused my efforts or reached out to my mentor. This program paired football players with a Christian mentor. That mentor would act as a spiritual guide and advisor. I wanted a partner that could help me in my walk of faith. I was paired with Daniel Hall, a local school principal. He and his wife are some of the most mild-mannered people you would ever want to meet. The sessions that we had were always intense and challenging. During this point of my freshman year, it was vital that I had someone to challenge me. His talks, along with former Clemson great Jeff Davis, led me to learn how to channel my emotions both on and off the field. Jeff Davis would always remind me in a humorous way that you never give anyone the keys to your car and let them drive you. Jeff was a former NFL player and pastor, and I valued each and every conversation that we had that year.

During this period of my life, God was positioning me for the blessings that were coming my way. I became hungry for greatness as a player, Christian, role model, and also in the classroom. Anything less was unacceptable. I was not going to settle. The search for identifying who I was before was now over. I knew that the things I had been through so early in my career were not a mistake, but instead a time for God to continue to cut the sides and shape this diamond. I had originally thought that redshirting my freshman year was a terrible loss, but now I realize it wasn't. It was all part of God's plan. This time allowed me to search for my identity.

My first year in college was full of obstacles and challenges, but in the end it helped me lay the foundation that would help create a legacy for me and my family, not only on Earth but in heaven as well. I'm hoping it is a legacy that lasts forever. It is crystal clear to me now that the injury was never a mistake, but it was a way for God to bless me and help me to grow. This growth is helping my vision become a reality. This was just another time for God to refine me in my spiritual journey.

7

BAPTISM BY FIRE

"Trust in the Lord with all your heart and lean not on your own understanding."

Proverbs 3:5. NIV

The year was 2008, and it was the second year of my collegiate journey. Because I had been redshirted during my freshman season, I was still considered a freshman on the field, but a sophomore in the classroom. I knew that I had to step up my game on the field, and also for the challenges of tougher classes. I knew much would be expected of me this year. As I lay in my quiet, dark room meditating, I could not help but think back about what had happened the previous year. That had been an eye-opening experience for me. I had grown so much in so many different ways: as a player, spiritually, and as a man.

The injury the previous season had taught me much about what to expect. I had learned that God was shaping me into what He wanted me to be. God had taken my circumstances and turned me into a leader, someone with the ability to inspire so many people, and that was humbling. I had learned never to take anything for granted. Football could be here one day and gone the next. I knew now that my true calling was to help people, and that would be on the football field as well as off.

The first evidence I had that my role was changing was during fall camp. I had recently won the starting middle linebacker position, beating out two other great players. Because I had beaten out a senior to claim the spot, it showed that I was highly regarded as a freshman. And it was not because I was the biggest or the fastest player, but it was because I practiced with relentless intensity. I had learned that if you really wanted something bad enough, you had to pursue it ceaselessly. This is not only true in football, but in life as well. The previous year, God had allowed me to go through many trials. God had allowed me to go through these so that I could become better, stronger. God wanted to see how badly I really wanted to achieve my goals. I had but one goal in camp, and that was to be the best player I could be. The hot days were draining, but I was able to dominate my competition. I also wanted to show the coaches that I was a changed man when it came to controlling my anger. I had finally learned how to channel my emotions in a positive manner, and I did this to honor God.

As I thought about winning the starting position, my phone started to ring. "Hello," I said. It was my mom. "Congratulations," she said in a cheerful voice. She was just as excited as I was. I had to smile but I reminded my mom that this was only the beginning. The tasks that lie before me would be difficult, and camp was only the beginning. I had won the respect of my coaches to earn the spot, but I still had to earn the respect of my teammates. I explained this to my mom, and she agreed. But she said, "I am excited for you and know you are going to do great things. Not that you need anything else to push you, but I do have a goal for you." "A goal?" I asked.

By this time, I started thinking to myself, what was my mom cooking up now? She is notorious for pushing me past my limit. But she only does it because she loved me, and wanted the best for me, and from me. My mind was working overtime to try to figure out what goal she had in her mind. She assured me that was exactly what she was saying. "Yes. Something else for you to work towards. God has not brought you this far to stop now. Life is not a sprint, it is a marathon. You always need another goal in front of you." "Okay mom, what do you have in mind?"

She said, "If you have an All-American season on the field, I will buy you a car." By this time, I was really smiling. But with my mom, I should have known that was not the end of it.

Then she came back and added, "But you also have to make all-conference academic team to get the car." That smile on my face quickly disappeared. I had never been a scholar, and I struggled even to qualify to come here. Now she was telling me that I had to be all-conference in academics? What kind of package deal was that? To qualify for the all-conference academic team, you had to have a certain amount of success on the field as well as in the classroom to qualify. As hard as it was going to be, I accepted the challenge. "You have a deal," I said. "I will make it happen." "All right then, make it happen son," she replied.

As soon as the conversation ended, I asked God for favor for all that I was going to try to do this season. I knew to accomplish all I wanted to, it was going to be a joint effort between me and God.

As the start of the season grew near, media interest in me started to pick up, and that was fine with me. Each year, just before the season begins, Clemson has a fan appreciation day. It is one of my favorite events. Fan day allowed me an opportunity to interact with all of the great Clemson fans that sat in our stands week after week, regardless of the heat, rain, or sleet. This fan day would be a little different for me. The previous year, I saw things from a different vantage point. I had just been an unknown football player from Mobile, Alabama. As I had looked from table to table, there were long lines before the star athletes and their autographs were in high demand.

I saw how much the fans respected them and I pointed out jokingly, "I see you superstars." Now, as I prepared for fan day, I had become that player. I was humbled by this whole experience. I remembered how people had said I would never take one snap at this level. It was definitely a new experience as people handed their babies over to me so they could take our picture. It was also a little strange because people were handing me their baby's arms or legs, asking me to sign them.

The first time that happened, I just stared at the lady with a blank look and said, "Are you serious?" She looked at me and laughed, "I am serious as a heart attack."

I was dumbfounded, but I eventually gave in to her request. Fans went from line to line in order to get autographs. I signed schedule posters, pictures fans had printed off from practice, helmets, and anything else you could imagine. I knew that day that my audience was growing, and my ability to impact others was starting to widen even before I took a snap.

Players, media, and coaches had created great anticipation before my first game. They wanted to see me perform on the big stage. I made sure to stay away from any magazines or press clippings during this time, because I wanted to stay grounded. I wanted to keep that same chip on my shoulder that I had carried all my life. It had always been my edge. Even though I tried to stay away, it was hard not to see the interviews that everyone kept telling me about. Everyone was calling me the steal of the 2007 signing class. Weeks before the first game, I had read an interview that one of the media sites had with Jarvis Jenkins, a defensive tackle. In this interview he praised my performance. They had picked a nickname for me, "Maintenance Maye."

I know it may sound funny, but earning that nickname meant a lot.

To me it was a sign that I was beginning to earn the respect of my teammates. He had used this term to describe my playing style. He said that if anyone was to miss a tackle, no matter how far from the line of scrimmage it was, Brandon Maye was going to take that ball carrier down. From that point on, and in every pre-season interview, the reporters used that nickname. As I said, I was honored by all of the positive comments. But I knew that nothing was going to come easy for me, and I had to work hard to achieve all of my goals.

Finally the week of the first game arrived. The excitement around campus, and through the fan base, was starting to really pick up. We had added to the expectations for the team when we signed a top 10 signing class headlined by the nation's number one recruit Da'Quan Bowers, the number one running back Jamie Harper, four-star tight end Dwayne Allen, cornerback Xavier Brewer, and offensive lineman Antoine McClain. Expectations were extremely high for our team and we began the season ranked at #9.

This was the day I had waited for all my life, and I had circled the date on the calendar. I tried to stay grounded and just wanted to view this as just one more game on the schedule, but in the back of my mind I knew this game was special. It was also very personal. The first game was against Alabama, which is one of the instate teams that had passed on me. Maybe they did not think I was good enough. But on Saturday, on the biggest stage in college football- College Game Day-I was going to get a chance in my first career start to prove to them that they had missed out on something special.

That week, I made sure I was accessible to all of the media guys. The coaches had taught me how to answer their questions. I knew there would be questions like, "Is this personal for you? Are you nervous about your first start? How do you prepare your mind to have your first start versus a SEC team?" That was definitely the type of questions I was asked all week.

"Well you know Alabama presents a tough test in so many ways for our team, so it's important we get off to a fast start," I responded all week. The coaches had taught me how to shy away from personal questions and give them what they wanted to hear, even if it did not exactly answer their question. I was always careful to compliment the other team in all of my interviews, and to raise my teammates up above myself.

Mike Herndon, a reporter from my hometown newspaper, did a phone interview with me that week. My boys called me about midway through the week and told me how the coaches had put up a quote from the interview saying I was trash talking. Though that never occurred, I learned that year that teams make up things you supposedly said to try to motivate their team. That is the life of being competitive in Division 1 football. After getting that message from my boys, I knew that I had to come with my A game. I would be baptized by fire this week. Even though it was my first start, I would have to shock the world and dominate during the game. I had to leave no doubt that Alabama had made a mistake by passing on me.

It was Friday, the day before I made my first career start. This week, I had the opportunity, in front of this crowd of at least 85,000 people and a worldwide audience on ESPN, to show the nation that I could be a force to be reckoned with on this level, despite what the coaches had said during my high school career. This game would be played in the beautiful city of Atlanta in the Georgia Dome. I had never been in the Dome before, but many people had told me it was a remarkable venue for college football games.

Emotions on this rainy Friday afternoon were a mixture of nervousness and excitement. This was evident through our final pregame planning meetings. Coach Vick was often long-winded during these meetings, but he knew his stuff and by the end of the meeting, I felt like I knew every one of their offensive players personally. Since I had been redshirted the previous season, all of the pregame meetings were new to me. The pregame events included meetings, meals, mental preparation, and the Tiger Walk. It was hard to believe that just a year before, I had watched the veterans so closely that I felt like I was already a four-year starter.

After eating, we stayed at our team facility. Before I knew it, it was time to head to our hotel in Atlanta. That was around 5. I rushed to grab my team issued Nike bag, and then went outside to be loaded on the bus. When I got outside, there were three buses. I was a little confused about which one to get on, until one of my teammates pointed me to the defensive bus. These buses were very roomy and luxurious. They were not at all like the Greyhound buses I had traveled on with my family as a child. Each seat had its own personal television set, but the only drawback was we had to watch whatever the seniors wanted to watch during road trips.

As we drove down the dark, lonely highways en route to Atlanta, the big lights from the escorting police cars startled me. My emotions were all over the place so, to calm them, I decided to meditate. By this time all of the others were in a deep sleep, but I took this time to visualize myself making plays and guessing what type of atmosphere this game would present. About an hour and a half after leaving Clemson, we turned into the Marriott parking lot on the busy streets of downtown Atlanta. I know all the people that were staying their thought the President was outside with all of the patrol cars that were escorting us. There were blinking blue lights everywhere.

That night, I was too excited to sleep. I was so ready to show all the people that had doubted me how good I was. Also the thought of my family traveling this late at night worried me. I tossed and turned all night long. My roommate for this game was senior Josh

Miller. By this time, all of this was familiar to him and he knew how to prepare. At one point that evening, he just grabbed the remote and turned it to ESPN. The first thing I saw was a commercial about College Game Day. That did nothing to calm my nerves. Throughout the evening hours, my adrenaline level was building. Sometimes I thought the morning would never come.

Finally daylight invaded our dark room, and I was the first to wake up. Since it was a late game, they would let us sleep until around 9:30 in the morning before heading to breakfast. I finally got to where I could not take it anymore; I felt like a caged dog. I gave up trying to sleep and went downstairs early just to sit in the lobby to have some coffee. I know they say that it is not good for athletes to drink coffee, but I continued to drink it. It reminded me of those early mornings with my grandma, reading her Bible at the kitchen table. Eventually the rest of the team came downstairs and we had breakfast. Many team coaches make breakfast like a memorial service, but this time we actually talked. Coach Bowden did not want us to be uptight, even though it was win or lose, with their job on the line.

For the rest of the day, we sat around the hotel watching television. Josh and I stayed in our room to watch College Game Day Live from the Georgia dome. It was so strange to me knowing soon we would be there. During the broadcast, Lee Caruso on the ESPN staff, started to analyze the game. I listened intently as I watched the segment on this large, 40-inch flat screen television. With most of the starters being returning players, the biggest question of the night would be how freshman linebacker, Brandon Maye, and the new junior linebacker would play during tonight's game. No one knows how shocked I was to hear my name coming from that television set! Later in my career, I would learn that both he and I had 100 tackles on the season, we had both earned all-conference honors, and we produced every game. It's funny to think now that we were labeled as the weak players. As I look back on it now, it seems funny that every year they would bring in a new, hotshot linebacker during recruiting to try to replace us but they never could.

As I watched the analysts that day, I noticed a shift in my mentality. It reminded me of a wolverine, because on the outside I would look calm, but on the inside my emotions were racing. I had to learn to just embrace the moment. It was now only about four hours before we would be heading to the stadium when I got a call from my mom, telling me they were in the lobby. I quickly rushed downstairs to greet my family, as they all stood wearing number 20 jerseys. I knew nothing about them getting the jerseys made, so that was a big surprise. My family has always been very supportive of me, and it turned into a trend for them to visit me on game days at the hotel. As time drew closer and closer for us to leave the hotel, my emotions were continuing to build. I put on my game face and headed alongside my teammates to load the bus to the Stadium. I could hear fans near the hotel cheering and chanting "C-L-E-M-S-O -N -T-I- G-E-R-S, Fight Tigers, Fight Tigers, Fight! Fight! Fight!" Every game we had a Tiger Walk, whether home or away. The fans were so passionate that, if we were at an away game, they would come to the hotel to perform the traditional Tiger Walk.

The ride to the Stadium was very exciting, and I sat in the back of the bus tapping my feet against the floor, keeping time to the beats that played through my headphones. I was so anxious for us to get to the Dome. I remember sitting in the back of the bus just to have a moment to pray to God and thanking him for this day. That day, it was hard for me to hold back the tears that were forming. I was crying tears of joy when I finally could see the Dome rising before us. I had never before experienced anything like this.

The roads were jammed with cars and it was hard to drive the buses through them, even with the police escort. No matter where you

DIAMOND IN THE ROUGH · BRANDON MAYE

looked out of the large tinted glass windows, there were people tailgating. I could see the smoke rise from their grills into the air. I could hear the sound from the fans dressed all in orange cheering, "Go Tigers." But it wasn't just Clemson fans in that parking lot. There were plenty of Alabama fans dressed in their Crimson as well, and they were saying anything but "Go Tigers". For some reason, seeing the fans tailgating really hyped me up. And, as strange as it may seem, it didn't matter if they were Clemson fans are Alabama fans. It all had the same effect. It not only got me, but everyone else on the bus, hyped up. The whole bus started to jump as we finally made the turn to go under the Stadium to the bus parking lot. As we pulled in, the bus got silent for a moment. All of the sudden, I could not hold it back anymore. I shouted out, "Let's go baby, it's show time!"

My teammates all looked at me like I was crazy, but they knew I was a hyper player and did everything with passion. My adrenaline was really flowing as we pulled our bags from under the bus and turned to walk through the door. I felt like I was walking down the red carpet at some hotshot award show. There were ESPN cameramen everywhere, trying to get a shot of every single player.

I had seen this many times before on television, but I had never experienced it myself. I had seen all the players, decked out in their suits, heading to the locker room. I had to ask myself, was this really happening to me right now? That's when it hit me. This was real. I was walking into the Georgia Dome, as a Division 1 starter. And I was about to play Alabama, one of the toughest teams in the nation. As I entered the Dome, I could clearly see the side view of the arena. I could see the big red seats, and the bright shining lights reflecting on the short cut turf.

This was probably the loudest crowd I had ever been a part of. Half of the fans were Clemson wearing their solid orange, and the other half were Alabama fans decked out in their crimson. Being a young player and wanting to impress my teammates and coaches, I expended about all of my energy during the pregame. It was now time for the game to start, and we exited the locker room after saying the traditional Lord's prayer. It was the first time I had been in the locker room on game day. I was one of the first players out of the locker room that day. I stood up proudly in front of the team, as we waited to run out of the tunnel. The emotions that had built throughout football camp for this moment really came to the surface. I had transformed into the ultimate warrior, and I was ready to explode as we ran out through the smoke to our sideline.

Alabama won the coin toss and had deferred to the second half. Our offense was on first. It was a quick three in, three out, as their defense was able to hold us. As I watched this, I knew we were up for a dogfight, as their stars Terrence Cody, Roland McCain, and Dont'a Hightower were making plays early. Now was the moment I had been waiting for all my life. It was finally time for me to take the field in my first game. It would have been natural for me to be nervous, but my adrenaline had already taken over. I rushed onto the field. It felt like all eyes were on me as I got down in my stance. I looked their quarterback, John Parker Wilson, directly in the eye. The ball was snapped, and I ran with everything in me towards their quarterback. "Boom!" I met running back, Glen Coffee, in the hole. My career had started off wonderfully, even though I had been thrown into the fire by playing my first game against an SEC football team like Alabama.

Watching the game, you would never have guessed that I was a freshman. I looked like a seasoned veteran, as I made plays all over the field. This really showed how far I had come, considering I had run the 40 yard dash initially at 5.4 seconds in high school. On the second possession, Alabama set up a screenplay to Julio Jones. He broke free of two would-be tackles and raced along the sideline

DIAMOND IN THE ROUGH · BRANDON MAYE

with no one left to beat. I had always been big on giving effort, and I would never give up on a play. This really paid off for the team big time, because I raced from my linebacker position, passed about three other players, to bring him down on their 40-yard line.

Coach Nick Saban had done a great job of preparing his players for the game. They were really beating us down, and we were down by 20 at the half. The score was 23 – 3. The only sign of life that we showed after half time was when CJ Spiller ran back the opening kickoff of the second half. But that spark quickly died, as Alabama capitalized on every play and eventually finished winning the game big, with a score of 34 – 10. Despite the score of the game, my career was off to an unbelievable beginning as I had made 12 tackles, and two for a loss. I was well on my way to breaking the Clemson single-game record with my first start, before coach bowed and pulled the starters during the beginning of the fourth quarter. That was not too bad for a person that many said would never play Division I football. But the game was also humbling as well, not only for me but for the rest of the team.

My next game experience would be at Death Valley. We were playing The Citadel. There were many mismatches during this game. This game could prove to be a tremendous confidence builder for our young players, or it could be a startling upset. Even though I, along with many other freshmen, were on the team, we set the tone early. It was a fast-moving game. Senior players like Mike Hamlin, Chris Clemons, and Chris Chancellor pushed me early. They were great role models and leaders, and I would pattern my behavior based on their example for years to come. There had been many times that season Mike Hamlin would single me out in the locker room. He challenged everyone to try to beat me to the ball. He knew that if they could, they were giving 100% on every play.

It was an amazing sight as our buses drove up to the Tiger walk. We exited the buses into a sea of orange, as the many fans gathered at the entrance to the stadium. If your heart was not pounding after the Tiger walk, you needed to have your vital signs checked, because you are probably not breathing. One thing that I learned that season was no matter who we were playing or what their record was, Death Valley was going to be rocking. Once again, I felt like I was dreaming as I stood at the top of the hill and looked out at all that orange. I had seen the videos of "running down the hill" on YouTube, but this was the first game I was going to be able to participate as a player. Unless you have experienced that yourself, you have no idea of the rush that you get when you rub that rock and charge down that hill. This game was over before it even started, as we quickly ran up the scoreboard and rested the starters during the second half. The following week, we were going to begin conference play by playing NC State.

The next week, I would encounter the first of many obstacles that would come that season. I had been diagnosed with a stomach virus that never seemed to go away. Our defensive line coach's wife, Kila Rumph, felt so guilty because I became violently ill after eating chili beans at her house that Sunday. She thought it was the beans that had made me sick, but I assured her that was not the case. I had a severe case of acid reflux, but I continued to eat everything that I wanted. Since I was away from home and shared my apartment with someone else who couldn't cook, I wanted to eat all of the home cooking I could handle. That entire week she would visit me throughout the day to bring medicine, soup, and Pedialyte. I really appreciated how she was treating me like one of her own children. Despite her heroic efforts to get me better by Wednesday so I could get some practice in, her valiant efforts failed. That whole week, I was doubled over in severe pain and still becoming violently ill. I thought it would never end.

The sudden illness had a positive impact on me, as it changed my eating habits. I was starting to take notice of everything that I put in my body. I had done this once before, and it certainly was beneficial to me then. I learned through Dr. Loretta Jackson, the team nutritionist, that my performance was based off what I put in my body. From that point on, I started a trend by inviting many of the players over to my apartment every week and using the cooking skills my grandmother had taught me. Many of them just called me a health freak, but that did not stop them from coming over. They usually said that with their mouth full of baked chicken or whatever else I had cooked that day.

The next two weeks presented us with a victory and a heart- breaker. We won our game against South Carolina State 54-0. Every Monday, the team would have a meeting with the coaches to read out the players' stats for each unit: offense, defense, and special teams. Then the players would receive a lifestyle poster that was a still shot of you from that game. The game against South Carolina State was a first for me, as I was selected as player of the game. It was a great honor, but it was quickly followed by a heartbreaking loss against Maryland. What made it so difficult was that we lost the game on the last play. For the entire game, we had been battling back and forth. We were one drive away from winning before Maryland had a reverse to their All-American wide receiver, Darius Heyward Bay, as he sprinted down the sideline for the winning touchdown. This loss was so heartbreaking because now, we would not be able to win our division. For a season that had started with so much promise, we were on a roller coaster ride. We now had three wins and two losses, and the wins were not against tough teams. That was definitely not an impressive resume for a team that had been ranked at #9 in the preseason.

That season, we were reminded of the quote, "it is not how you started, but instead how you finished." I really wish that we could have reversed that statement that season and finished the way we started, but that was not to be. It was about to go from bad, to worse. I was personally crushed because I had expected to have a huge freshman season, as I had been named, along with linebacker Donta Hightower from Alabama and Oklahoma's Travis Lewis, as the National Midseason Freshman.

There were many times throughout the season that I experienced many freshman mistakes, but for the most part, I was making plays that were overshadowing those mistakes. My fame was growing, and it became tougher for me to go to local restaurants with family or friends without being asked for my autograph or someone taking my picture. As we got ready to travel to Wake Forest with a 3–2 record, we had no idea how much things were going to change for the rest of the season. Clemson University was known for always having a winning season, and making it to the best bowl games. And it was up to our head coach, Tommy Bowden, to make that happen again. If, as head coach, you did not meet those expectations, you would find yourself in the hot seat with your job on the line. There was a real chance that coach Bowden would get fired that season. I guess I was a little naïve, because I never really paid any attention to those rumors in the locker room. Most of the other players did not either. We had heard that so many other times that we did not give it a second thought. Looking back on it now, maybe we should have. Thinking back on it, I never really understood because the fans still came out and supported us in droves. I thought happy fans meant that the coach's job was secure. Those rumors went in one ear and out the other.

Those rumors actually came true after a loss on a Thursday night. After that loss, Tommy Bowden was fired. There had been conflicting reports when everyone heard the news. Some reports said that he had stepped down; others said he was fired. Some said that coach Bowden was fired because he had been so loyal to his assistant, because he refused to fire our offensive coordinator, Rob

Spence. The bottom line is that we were a 3 – 3 team. There was an emergency team meeting called to tell us the news. The news quickly turned viral. I really didn't understand why they fired him because he had always been a good head coach. He was mild-mannered, respectful, and smart. I still remembered when he recruited me, sitting in our living room with no shoes on. He had been one of the main reasons I had come to Clemson. But now, he was gone. I am a firm believer that the players are the ones who actually control the scoreboard, not the coaches.

The team meeting started with the athletic director, Terry Don Phillips, coming in to address the team, letting us know what had happened. At the end of the meeting, we were introduced to the interim coach Dabo Swinney, who was serving as the wide receiver coach on Tommy Bowden's staff. Dabo was a coach I had been around for a while. During the past year, when I was on the scout team, I remembered going against his offense. I remembered we had run-ins when I hit Jacoby Ford, his star receiver, and he had gotten a concussion. He hated when I would go near his wide receivers, because he knew I was going to hit them, and hit them hard. It did not matter which drill or segment of the practice we were in.

Coach Swinney is a little different than Coach Bowden. He was more like your Paul Bear Bryant type of coach. Instead of being laid-back, watching on the sidelines, his voice was always echoing across the practice fields. It was a battle to keep him off the field during practice. I watched him set the pace for practice, and how he drove his wide receivers. They constantly had to be going full out. If they didn't, it could be guaranteed that Coach Sweeney would be out on the field hollering at them. I had personally never been coached by Coach Swinney, outside of hearing him hollering at me for hitting his wide receivers.

Coach Swinney's wife, Kathleen, is a real sweetheart. She always has a kind word and a soft, gentle voice. They had three young sons. There was one son in particular that was always around the players, almost like an assistant. His other son, Will, was definitely a genius. This kid could write all of the president's names, backwards, if you wanted him to. Coach Swinney was also from the state of Alabama, and I knew he was on the 1992 National Championship team at the University of Alabama. He had lettered in three teams after coming in as a walk on. This made me respect him, because of the similarities in our stories.

As soon as Coach Swinney began to speak, I could tell there was a sense of nervousness about him. I think he was just as shocked as we were. Yesterday, he had been just a wide receiver coach; now he was standing before us, addressing the team as the head coach.

He did not waste any time, as he started in a sad manner, "Okay, men first off, I am as deeply saddened about Coach Bowden as I know you are." He paused for a minute and sniffled a little. You could tell he was fighting mixed emotions. He was both excited about the opportunity to be the head coach, and sad about Coach Bowden's situation. But suddenly, his voice changed. He started sounding like a head coach, "I am so humbled and grateful for Terry Don passing this team on to me. I only know one way to do this, and I have to put my own spin on things," referring to his style of coaching and the way he went about things. Coach Swinney gave everybody the option to leave if you were not "ALL IN." He shared with us that "ALL IN" was not just a slogan, but a way of life. That was the first time I had heard that slogan and many coaches since then began using it when addressing their team. Coach Dabo then told us his life story. He told us how he had been a former walk on that ended up earning a scholarship. He told us that he was just a poor kid that grew up in Alabama. His story was so inspirational, that I think everyone left the meeting "ALL IN".

Outside our team facility that day, media from all over the world were camped out. The scene was completely chaotic. Coach Bowden had been the head coach at Clemson for a very long time by this point, and his name was really popular since his dad was one of the winningest coaches in college football, at Florida State. Their family is like football royalty. I was a young freshman then, and I was just starting to get used to the program. It did not make sense to me that after all he had done for the program, it could end so suddenly. I was saddened by this, and I did not understand everything then. This situation is not uncommon in Division I football; every year coaches are fired. That is simply the nature of the business. But as a freshman, it was devastating.

The next week, there was so much media attention surrounding our team. Earlier that week, the team had been held from interviews, but eventually they were allowed to give interviews as they were leaving practice. The atmosphere of that first Monday practice was gloomy. I recalled walking to my locker room after Monday night practice. It was very sad. You would have thought that Coach Bowden had passed on, as camera crews stood at the steel gated entrance waiting for us to exit the practice field that day. I only did a few interviews because I had a very big test the next day, but I could see many of the players were actually crying as they left the field, and addressed the media about coach Bowden.

By the next week, the players had started to adjust to Coach Swinney's style. After hearing that Coach Swinney had come basically from the same situation I had-a small town in Pelham, Alabama-to having a chance to be the head coach at Clemson University, I respected him very much. I have always been moved by inspirational stories like that, because it reminded me of my journey and it kept me grounded. I knew I was "ALL IN", and fighting to save our season. But I, along with many teammates, also wanted to make sure that Coach Swinney got the job permanently. I knew it would be a financial boost for him and his family, and it would be a dream come true after all his hard work. He had not gotten this job because he wanted it, but we all felt he deserved it.

It was easy to see the crowd was rejuvenated, as we took on Georgia Tech in Death Valley that Saturday. It was obvious what my family had told me was true. They had told me that there was a new excitement in the air. I witnessed this firsthand when I saw the biggest crowd I had ever seen during our traditional Tiger Walk. I knew it was going to be a tough battle between us and the other team, as both teams threw punches. None was more powerful than the last one Georgia Tech threw, with five minutes to go in the half. Georgia Tech's new head coach, Paul Johnson, was known for his triple option offense. They were on our 30-yard line. Their quarterback faked the ball and our whole defense bit. I turned to look from my linebacker spot, as the ball went into the air. I remembered saying to myself, "NOOOOOO." Their quarterback, Josh Nesbitt, found a wideopen Demetrius Thomas for the touchdown. This was a tough loss because of all of the emotions that had taken place that week.

The next couple of weeks would be huge for me. As we entered our bye week, my young body was starting to feel the demands of being a starter in the ACC. That couple of weeks would also give us time to adjust to coach Swinney, and the way he did things. The whole team had felt like they had been caught up in a whirlwind since the firing of Coach Bowden. Over the next two weeks, we had to identify what type of legacy the 2008 team would leave behind. There were only a few games left, and we had a record of 3 – 4.

Since I did not have a car at the time, I always hitched a ride with my teammate, Jock McKissic, to his Opelika, Alabama home, where I was picked up by my parents. It was wonderful to be home to spend time with my family. Because they traveled up for games, I often got the chance to see my mom, stepdad, sisters, and then girlfriend Jennifer Johnson, who came every chance she could between her demanding volleyball schedule at Albany State and classes. But there was one lady that had played a huge part in my life that I did not get to see that entire summer; it was my grandma. She could not travel those long roads because of her age and health. Every morning of my three-day visit, me and my grandmother would gather there at the table and catch up on life, while we drank a cup of coffee, though I was careful not to consume too much because I did not want to alter my performance.

The trip ended all too soon, and before I realized it, I was back in my room studying the game plan for the Boston College game. Since it was an away game, this would be the first game of my career that I would not have my mom at the game. I knew this would be weird, when I looked out into the crowd and could not spot her lovely face, and see her prideful smile. She had always lectured me throughout my childhood that there were going to be times in life that she was not going to be there. I understood the process of leaving the nest and becoming a man, but there was nothing in the world like having my mother's touch. She did tell me that she would take off work that day, and would be watching every snap which offered me some comfort.

There was something else that was bothering me about that game. It was the plane ride. It did not matter whether I was the first, second, or 10th person loading the airplane, I was still nervous. This would be the first plane trip I had taken with the team, and flying was a challenge for me. For some reason, I always thought about the September 11 tragedy. I still remember watching the news, when the two planes crashed into the World Trade Center. Then, just as now, that is always on my mind when I board an airplane. This was only my second plane ride; the first one had occurred during my first official visit to Clemson. The difference was that plane had been small, and this huge, Delta plane really reminded me of those 9/11 airplanes.

I knew no matter what, that if I wanted to play in the game, I was going to have to board that airplane. I looked around at all of my teammates, staff, coaches, and their wives, and no one else looked nervous. I had waited in my line patiently but at the last minute, I made a run for it. I thought if I acted like I had to go to the restroom that would give me time to collect my thoughts. Unfortunately the coaches read my mind and sent a grad student after me. I remember saying, "No! No! I'm not getting on that plane!" Needless to say, moments later, I was in my small seat with a frightened look on my face.

That Boston College game provided us with the confidence to finish our season strong. We had won yet another nail-biter. We finish the season winning three of our last five games, including the one that meant the most to us. We won against our in-state rivals, South Carolina. After that huge victory over the Gamecocks, fans had connected with Dabo Swinney. At the end of the game, all of the fans were chanting, "Dabo! Dabo Dabo!" until the clock ran out. Dabo had a different philosophy that involved getting the student body involved with football, and also getting his team members out into the community. It didn't matter if we were reading books to elementary school students or passing out canned goods, he encouraged us to do it with pride. We were, after all, Clemson Tigers. Not only had he won over the fans, he won over the athletic director as well. A couple of days later, he was hired as the new head football coach. He quickly made changes to his staff, firing both the offensive coordinator and defensive coordinator. He then hired Alabama's Kevin Steele, as the defensive coordinator, and Billy Napier, who was already on staff, to be in charge of the offense.

My freshman season had been a roller coaster ride. As a fresh- man I had been thrown into the fire in so many ways. But it also helped me mature. I had learned how to prepare for games, balance my football and my studies, and it prepared me to make transitions in my future. But above all that season, I learned to lead. In my first season as a rookie, my performance was far from that of a freshman. I started 12 games that season. After a close race between me and Miami's Sean Spence, I came in second place by only a few votes for the ACC Defensive Rookie of the Year. I had the best stats of any freshman in the conference. But, the ultimate reward was proving to the world that I was worthy of starting on a Division I football team like Clemson. I recorded 90 tackles that season, which was the most by any freshman since Anthony Simmons in 1995. To add to my stat sheet, I registered five tackles for a loss, two sacks, and a team-high of 10 quarterback pressures.

That season, I led all freshmen in the ACC and tackles. I subsequently earned All American National by FWAA's Freshman, All American, and College Football News' All-Freshman team. I had accomplished more than any man outside of my family believed that I could. Through faith, and working hard, I had achieved all of the goals I had set. There were few people willing to go through what I had, from high school recruiting, heartbreaks, being talked about, doubted, and mistreated, to persevere and conquer that high goal. I would receive another major boost that year, because I was soon riding around campus in my new 2008 silver Dodge Charger. After I had fulfilled my promise of being selected to the All-ACC academic team, my mom kept up her end of the bargain. Even though she was struggling financially, she bought me the car as promised. I really don't know if it was the car, or if it was just me, but now I understood that football is like life; it is never promised. I would eventually make the all-academic team for two seasons. There is no greater reward for a person than to make up in their mind they are going to make it through. I had won through my work ethic. At the end of the season, I walked to the stage at the annual banquet, smiling yet humble. I knew that this was only the beginning. God had more chapters to write in this testimony.

My first fan day in 2008,
sharing the moment with two special people.

It wouldn't be possible if it was not for Coach Blackwell
believing in me as a person and player.

Making plays vs Alabama. The most tackles by a Clemson freshman since Anthony Simmons in 1995.

Big goal line stop vs Maryland 2008.

Big slam vs our rival, South Carolina.
Rest in Peace Kenny McKinley.

8

A SEASON TO REMEMBER

"I figure life's a gift and I don't intend on wasting it. You don't know what hand you're gonna get dealt next. You learn to take life as it comes at you... to make each day count."

Leonardo Di Caprio, Titanic

With the success of my first year on the field and in the classroom, I knew I did not want to become complacent. I knew I also had to remain grounded. I knew that I was not a freshman anymore, and more would be required of me. I had to keep in mind that last season was simply that, last season. In order to become a true champion, I had to push myself harder than ever. Personally, I expected more of myself. I also knew that my team would be looking for me to give more this season on the field, in the classroom, in the community, and during the off-season summer workouts.

During the summer workouts, I focused on being a leader by example. I could not ask anyone to do anything I was not willing to do myself. I knew I also had to become more vocal and begin developing a voice that commanded respect from my other teammates. I not only wanted to add something special to my game, I wanted to add something special to theirs as well. I wanted to make my team better. I had learned through experience with the team, that as individuals you could do nothing. But as a team, you could defeat anything. I often thought of my mentor, Ray Lewis illustration using your hand. He explained to me that if you spread your hand out and try to bend each finger down; it was easy because they are individual fingers. But when you made a fist (referring to a team) it is impossible to pull your fingers away. I wanted our new coaches and my teammates to understand that I could be trusted to lead. At any time, when addressing my team, I spoke life.

Workouts were tougher than ever. It was obvious that coach Batson was intensifying things. He was trying to change the culture, after a disappointing previous season. I really thought that we were training for the Olympics, as much as we ran. There were always players lying on the ground after every run, losing what they had eaten that day. Even though these workouts were challenging, it made me want to drop to the ground myself, but my pride would not allow me to do so.

The summer was divided into two parts: first summer session and second summer session. We would receive a break in between, and would report back on the 4th of July or the day before. I never really understood that, but by this time I had my own transportation. Every opportunity and every chance I got, I would go home. At the end of the first summer session, we were given a two-week break. I went home unaware that something would happen during this visit that would make me value the gift of life even more.

It was a sunny afternoon, July 2nd, and my family and I were sitting around the kitchen table eating and talking. It was a pre- Fourth of July celebration. I had spent most of the day with my family, and later decided to go visit my girlfriend in the Toulminville Community, which was on the other side of town. She lived on a quiet street, full of elderly people with little to no traffic. I stayed at her house for about two hours and left around 10 o'clock that night. I knew that there had been several carjacking's in the area, and more than one death. Because of this, I made sure I was alert and aware of my surroundings. I knew I didn't want to stay out there too late. I had so many positive things going on in my life that I did not want anything negative to happen.

Even though I knew I was going to be going through a rough part of town, I knew I was covered by God's blood. Even knowing this, I was still very careful. As I drove from her house, through the dark neighborhoods, I grew very sleepy. It had been a very long day, and I decided to take what I thought would be a faster route to my house. Trying to get home quickly, I passed near LeFlore High School in an attempt to get onto the interstate. As I came up by the school, I made a turn down a small-lighted street beside the school. As I was listening to music, suddenly I heard a "Pop! Pop! Pop." I turned down my music to make sure my ears were not deceiving me. They were not. Though I tried to convince myself it wasn't, I knew it was gunshots. I looked around, but I did not see anyone on the vacant streets. Nothing seemed out of the ordinary, so I continued to drive toward my house. Since it was around July 4th I thought it was just some kids shooting off fireworks early.

Out of nowhere, a black Escalade appeared behind me with their bright lights on. Again I heard the distinct sound of gunshots. They were getting closer. All of the sudden, I saw the gunfire coming out of the back window of the Escalade. My heart started pounding. All I could think about was how my father had died. I knew I was in a race for my life, so I floored it. All of the sudden, one of the shots met its mark and broke out one of my taillights. I knew my car had been hit and I knew they meant business. Racing through the streets, I figured they must have mistaken my car for someone else. I knew I had better get out of harm's way.

While swerving in and out of traffic, my life started to flash before my eyes. I could see myself sitting in front of the television that Super Bowl Sunday, I thought of my Pop Warner football days, of high school, and about college. And of course, I thought about what my death would do to my family. All of the sudden, there was something white, cloudy, and bright shining in my eyes. At that time, I did not have time to analyze what was going on. As I think back on it now though, I know that it was God. God was protecting me.

I remember heading toward a fork in the road, as shots were coming from the black Escalade and drawing ever closer. My decision had to be quick, and I would have to live with whatever happened or die trying. The entire time I prayed to myself, "Please, let them go the opposite way Lord." The Lord answered my prayers as I wildly turned left, and the black Escalade continued right. I knew I was fortunate to be alive. There had been a lot of shots flying, and I was surprised that they had hit my car only once. I knew without a doubt that God spared my life on this night, and I also knew that the season to come was going to be a special one, one to remember. After this experience of being chased, shot at, and nearly killed, I was ready to return to South Carolina. I wanted something better than being chased around town and dodging bullets. At Clemson University, I knew that I was safe. Besides classes and football, the closest that I would come to an adventure would be dodging a large deer standing on the dark roads or being chased off somebody's farm for trespassing. I was relieved to know that I did not have much to worry about in Clemson. Clemson was my home away from home.

At Clemson, we had a new coaching staff. This would be a new season. This season meant a new beginning for me. Nothing that happened the year before mattered. I was prepared and ready to fight for the starting position again. My new coach was Kevin Steele. I knew Coach Steele well from his days at Alabama. Coach Steele was always a highly emotional coach and taught with plenty of fire and passion. I thought he wanted players that were vocal and fervent, but he wanted players to be smooth, calm, and confident. He wanted players who were focused on the task at hand. He was not really a fan of celebrating on the field after making plays. He wanted us to celebrate with our teammates. I would have to work hard to adjust to his coaching style because I played the game with so much hunger, that I get lost in myself sometimes.

When asked why I celebrate so much during games, I normally respond, "Coach, we would not win if I did not celebrate a little. I am not trying to make everybody look at me. You have got to understand something. You only know the glory, but you have no idea the struggle it took for me to get here."

Coach Swinney made an announcement during our first team meeting that everyone was even, and that during camp, every position was an open position. After Coach Swinney spoke, many of the guys in the locker room laughed out loud. Some understood that despite the coach's words, there were no openings for the positions of players like CJ Spiller, Jacoby Ford, and many of the other marquee players. Coach Swinney had torn a page out of Nick Saban's book over the summer with those comments. The team, however, appreciated the sentiment. We all knew we had to work hard to win. We all figured that you had to learn from the best to be the best, and we were fired up.

Coach Dabo was boldly out to change what we had done in the past. The change he orchestrated came early in camp, with the addition of more physicality and tempo in the practices. He did not mind starting over periods of workouts if guys were not giving enough effort. His style of coaching and approach to the game was tough. At first, many of the veterans had to adjust to the changes, but eventually we all bought in. By the end of camp we were sold out. This team did not look like the previous team, despite the large number of veterans. We had a lot of uncertainty. There were several question marks. First, our All Conference Quarterback, Cullen Harper, graduated and left the team. We had a redshirt freshman, Kyle Parker, as the listed starter. The offensive line had to replace at least three starters. No one knew what to expect. I simply focused on what I had to do for Clemson to be successful on the field. I knew that either Kavell or Maye would become Butkus Award Winners this season, if we worked hard, but even that was a big question mark.

After a challenging camp, and making the necessary adjustments to fit into the new defense, which was based off NFL philosophies, I won the starting position. Earning the starting role meant a weekly meeting with Coach Kevin Steele. I would now be the "Defensive Peyton Manning." I would be in charge of making calls and checks based on formations. Coach Steele had encouraged me earlier when he said that I played the run as good as Rolando McClain. It was quite a compliment to me because McClain was a First Round NFL Linebacker. The things that stood out most to me about McClain were the way in which he studied the game of football and how smart he was in the defense package. I desired to be that type of player.

During the pre-season, my teammate and fellow linebacker, Stanley Hunter, was told that he would have to give up football due to epilepsy and his increasing number of seizures. I dwelled on Stanley's situation for a while, and thought about it during my prayer sessions. It was really sobering. I found it upsetting as I realized that a guy who had given his all in every workout, in every practice, and in every game, had been forced to give up the game of football for life. The situation reaffirmed to me the fact that football does not last forever. You never know when your last play or practice will come. I prayed for Stanley often and, after meditating on everything that had happened to him, I decided to do something special to honor his loyalty and commitment. My mother was the first person I told before going to Coach Swinney and asking him if I could wear his jersey number 17 in the first game against Middle Tennessee State. Coach Swinney did not blink twice before calling the equipment room and getting "Maye" put on the back of a #17 orange game jersey. My mother was as excited as many of the fans that I was going to represent #17 in the season opener, and they quickly called it the Grand Gesture. The slogan quickly spread to my family as they got shirts printed up with my picture on it that read: Grand Gesture for the game. After that game, the wearing of Stanley's jersey number spread throughout the team. Other players took turns wearing the #17 jersey throughout the season. I believe this opportunity to be special, a time in my life where God gave me the opportunity to be a servant, and allowed me to do something to lift someone else up, instead of myself. The gesture was small, but it meant a lot to Stanley. I also learned the importance of each day. Events like this one were vital to me as I was developing into a man. I consider them polishing stages in the process of producing a shiny diamond.

The first game against Middle Tennessee State was a very emotional one for me. I played in this particular game with a different level of dedication. I had no idea what had gotten into me. I had become known for making plays, but on this night, I completely dominated in my position. It felt like the number 17 was magical. During the whole game, all I thought about was Stanley, who was over on the sideline smiling hard. I finished the game with 14 tackles, 1 sack, 1 interception, and caused a fumble. I was named Defensive Player of the Game by the Clemson Coaching Staff and, on the following Monday, I was named Defensive Lineman of the Week in the Atlantic Coast Conference. After the game, Stanley and I met near the gate that leads us to the locker room for photos. One of the photographs taken of me and Stanley, standing side-by-side, was used to make a life-sized player of the game poster, and it was given to both of us as a keepsake. I was just excited to have something that would help me remember that day forever.

After the 37-14 win over Middle Tennessee State, we lost 3 out of our next 5 games. We lost to Georgia Tech, TCU, and Maryland. There was not as much hype at the start of this season as with previous years, but we were working towards a common goal, and that goal was to play for the ACC Championship. Losing two conference games early had dimmed our chances of achieving our goal, but there was something that was a little different about our team. The 2009 Clemson Football Team had genuine leadership. Those who led did so with conviction and outworked others. There were not many guys trying to put on a front for the coaches when it came to playing time. Playing time was earned. The talent level did not compare or come close to the previous team at Clemson, but this team was hungry. When we entered into our bye week, after the Maryland game; we simply sat back and refocused on our goal.

This bye week meant a little more to me than normal, as I went through X-Rays and MRIs. I had taken a cheap shot from a Maryland player, near our sideline during the game, and that incident would change me forever. This was my first injury since fall camp freshman year. The hit from the side caused me to start having stingers regularly, but I would never tell anybody about them. When we returned from the open date, I went to the locker room and found that an old school, Dick Butkus type of horse collar was added onto my pads. I quickly rushed to the training room to see what this was for. The training room staff informed me that it was to be used for precautionary reasons. I was told that I had to play with this. At practice that week, it was the most humiliating thing I had ever had to wear. It immobilized my neck and made me a stiff player. Danny Poole, the trainer, eventually got me a smaller collar, but there was really no change. The collar took away from my aggressive style of play and made me more robotic. I complained to everyone to no avail. Dabo, Steele, and Jeff Davis all gave me the same answer. The collar stayed on if I wanted to play football. Though disappointed, I was not surprised. Sometimes I wonder what role Jeff Davis had in requiring me to wear this type of collar, because it had been popular when he played football. It was frustrating wearing a collar, but I wore it for my own good.

Open dates had always been good for this Clemson team. The last two seasons, we played our best games off of open dates. Every player reported back to campus with the swagger of an undefeated team. I was amazed because, initially I thought that the leaders would have to step to the front, and challenge the guys. But everyone returned focused and excited about getting back to work. Whatever happened during the time off motivated the team. The excitement and focus flourished on the football field that week when we destroyed Wake Forest 38-3. Monday after the game, my teammates joked with me about my collar. Someone said I looked like the guy from Austin Powers who put his shoulders to his ears and shouted, "Turtle, Turtle." I laughed it off because I thought it was funny too. Besides, I could not do anything about it if I wanted to play football. I jokingly suggested that they should trademark the collar. With the exception of me and my teammates, no one really cared about the collar anyway.

In our next game, we played Miami. This was one of the most thrilling games I had ever played in. If you stared at the scoreboard, you would have thought it was broken because the score was constantly changing. Since I played on the defensive unit, this was not a great thing for me. We won in double overtime 40-37. The victory came after Jacoby Ford made a catch in the end zone and we, the defense, stopped them on all four downs. The whole team stormed the field as Ford brought in the game winning catch. I believe that after this victory, our team realized its potential and we were determined now, more than ever, to play for the ACC Championship. I had 8 tackles that day, and a huge forced fumble in the 3rd quarter to set up a critical score from our offense. Despite being reduced to a robotic man by the collar, I was a sophomore leading my team.

And I knew I was catching the eye of NFL scouts. It was surreal time in my life.

After the victory over Miami, we found ourselves in the position to win our side of the conference. There were three conference games left: Florida State, North Carolina State, and Virginia. We were doing all the right things at the right time of the season. The team was motivated and re-charged after winning some close games; games designed to make or break teams. Well, those victories made our team. We defeated Florida State 40-24, and North Carolina State 43-23. The two victories renewed our team's hope in achieving our goal of playing in the ACC Championship. We controlled our own destiny. We were in second place in the division, and we had Boston College, who we had beaten earlier in the season, in front of us at number one. To play for the ACC Championship, we needed to win big at home in Death Valley.

Getting into the title game was not that complicated. With a victory over Virginia, there would be an outright tiebreaker with Boston College. With our previous victory over Boston College earlier in the season, we would win the tiebreaker. We would also get a shot if Boston College were to lose their game to North Carolina. The situation made me think of what my mom always reminded me of as a young man, "Control the things you can control and the rest will work itself out, if it's to be." As a leader on the team, and lead tackler going into the biggest game of the year thus far, I made sure when I spoke to the team that my message was centered on that. I wanted every player to understand that if we won the game against Virginia, we were heading to the ACC Championship.

Making it to the ACC Championship Game would be huge for the team, university, and devoted fans. Not only would that give us an opportunity to get a ring, but also a chance to gain a life lesson. There are many times in life where you are knocked down at the start of something, but it's important that you don't wallow in self-pity when you are down; instead, you dust yourself off and continue to fight the good fight of faith. I have been reminded many times about what was said earlier in the season, and during my life that, "It is not how you start, but rather how you finish things."

Practice that week was full of excitement, and I could just feel that sense of hunger for victory in my teammates. It was evident even during our stretching periods at the start of practice, as loud music played through the speakers on the practice field. It was evident in my body language, which Coach Steele said showed everything, that the music loosened any tightness that came during the week of preparation for our shot at the title. It is fair to say that Coach Dabo's method of playing modern music as well as oldies was paying off for the team. When I looked into the eyes of my teammates, it was like looking into the eyes of a tiger as he stalked his prey. We were all very focused. If the energy and tempo of that practice that week was any indication of how the game would be played on Saturday, I knew Virginia was in big trouble. There was never a doubt in my mind of what the outcome would be. We had the support of highly devoted fans, and as an added bonus, it would be Military Appreciation Day. As our fans honored our troops, it would make the game even that much more special.

As we arrived at the stadium, there was an enthusiastic crowd dressed all in orange waiting for us at the Tiger Walk. You could gauge the anticipation for kickoff by the shouts coming from all of the fans. This was the first game that I intentionally hurried into the locker room. I embraced a few friends and made sure I gave my family members their hugs as they stood in front of the Cash's tent. These people were very supportive, close friends, and diehard Clemson fans.

As I walked into the locker room, I thought about all of my previous coaches from Pop Warner to now, that always told me that it did not matter what the other team did. What mattered was what I did. What mattered most at that moment was that a win against Virginia meant that we could play for the ACC Championship. The thought of Boston College losing was irrelevant. I wanted us to get in on our own merits. I wanted us to win this game. We were not banking on North Carolina winning, but we were human, and the human and certainties and doubts were kicking in as many of us rushed into the facilities on this particular day.

Although it was a loose atmosphere in the locker room, if you desired to listen to your own music, you had to do so through your own personal headphones. This was done out of respect for each players' different preparation regiments. The Clemson locker room is completely different from what I had the opportunity to see when I would later attend Mississippi State. Music was always blasted through two DJ style speakers, from the time we arrived to the time we left. But today was different. On this day, both televisions were turned off. I guess Coach Swinney understood human nature, and knew that we would be watching the Boston College North Carolina game, instead of focusing on the task at hand. Many of the players were already a step ahead of Coach Swinney though, and many had watched the televisions in the training room. The lines that was usually thin and quick to get taping jobs done before a game moved much slower today. Everyone was trying to get a glance at the scoreboard of the North Carolina Boston game. As we went out for pre-game warm-ups, the half-time score showed North Carolina up 21-10.

Moments after returning from warm ups and loading the bus to ride around to the hill, we all knew that we were heading to the ACC Championship Game.

As Coach Swinney walked into the locker room to give us our

pre-game speech, he congratulated us on becoming the Atlantic Division champions of the ACC saying, "Men, your hard work paid off. Congratulations! We are heading to the Championship Game." After that, he then made sure we understood something important, and in an excited voice, with no smile on his face he insisted, "Make no bones about it, clinching a ticket to the title game, does not mean that we do not go out and dominate tonight."

He then started going over things that we had to do well to win the game; stressing the term tanoga -"take aways, no give aways," referring to the offense protecting the football and the defense creating turnovers. He then concluded after everyone in the locker room recited the Lord's Prayer, "Let's make sure there is a party in the Valley tonight! Let's listen men...hey...listen, here...let's show the world the true meaning of ACC (Atlantic Coastal Conference). He then smiled for a quick second and said, "Another Clemson Championship."

That night there was certainly a party in the Valley. In fact, I started the party. Virginia, not surprisingly, attempted to run the ball right at me on the first play of the game. I believe teams still thought that a mere two-star sophomore was not going to make plays. The misguided thought of those teams and coaches only meant more plays made by me at the end of the day. They came out in the I-formation, which meant two running backs and one as the lead blocker. They snapped the ball and, before anyone knew it, I was meeting the Virginia running back, Rashawn Johnson, in the hole. The hit was so violent the ball shot out heading one way and his body another. My teammates and the crowd went crazy screaming. The play was the tone setter that sent a message. We were not just going to the title game, but we were there to take care of business tonight.

Not only did that start set the tone for the team and the crowd, but it was the start of a special night for me. The game was a battle with scoring back and forth. The halftime score was 31-24. Virginia was a team that did not have much to lose. Virginia was heading to a bowl game, and they wanted to spoil the party for us. Virginia used all kinds of trick plays: Reverse plays, Quarterback throwbacks, and Play Actions. If there was a trick play within the rules in the game of football, I believe Virginia ran it that night. All of that was good until Coach Steele got us into the locker room and drew up some counter attack plays for the second half. I must say the plays worked because Virginia was shut out the second half- not scoring any points. The final score to the game was 31-24. The win was a huge victory for many people. As the crowd rushed the field after the game, the song, "We Will Rock You," played loudly in the stadium.

Like so many other times in my life, I wanted to share this special one with my family. My family is my support and encouragement, and they had sustained their faith in God, and in me. After about 30 minutes, I finally fought my way through the huge crowd that covered the field to get to them. It was tough. There were reporters trying to grab me for interviews, fans wanting autographs, and some people there asking for my helmet, which belonged to the school. I could see my mom and sisters in the distance smiling, as I made my way through the crowd to them.

I quickly rushed towards my mom and said these words, "We did it! What a comeback to a slow starting season? We are playing for it all!"

She was just as excited as I, and tears ran down her face. I knew the thoughts she was having; thoughts of how good God was for this opportunity, and how great God was for allowing me to be a part of something special. This was one of those times during the journey that I felt as if I were dreaming. There would be many more to come, I thought to myself.

The only bad thing about this victory over Virginia and advancing to the ACC Championship, was that we now had two weeks before the title game. And before the championship, we had the next biggest game of the year. Every season we play our in-state rival, South Carolina. I was very knowledgeable about in-state rivalry games. In the State of Alabama, you chose your side at birth, between the University of Alabama and Auburn University, and everyone looks forward to the Iron Bowl. The Iron Bowl in Alabama is one of the biggest rivalry games in the country, and it seems to get bigger every year. Growing up in Alabama, it was larger than life to some people. The trash talking was year-round, and a loss meant you had to be on the receiving end of the joke. I never really was in to the rivalry thing as a player. I simply focused on the next game on the schedule. Over my first two seasons at Clemson, I had learned and been brainwashed to dislike South Carolina, or else. By this time, my red-shirted sophomore year, I was a serious part of the anti-Gamecock team. I think that if some of the fans had to choose between winning the ACC championship or beating the Gamecocks, there is no doubt in my mind that a victory over the Gamecocks would prevail.

The players and the coaches at Clemson understood how important beating the South Carolina Gamecocks was. It was a matter of pride. The importance of this game was stressed heavily throughout the week of preparation. It was evident to me that we did not have the same energy as the previous week. I, and probably most of my teammates, were already focused on the trip to Tampa for the ACC championship game against Georgia Tech. Our minds were all over the place. Our lack of focus was evident that Saturday as we traveled to Columbia, South Carolina for the big rivalry game.

The atmosphere was that of a typical South Carolina vs. Clemson rivalry game. The fans in Columbia let us know from the moment of our arrival into the stadium that we were not welcome there.

They threw beer on our buses, and made all kinds of unwelcoming gestures towards us. It was a very hostile environment to say the least, but we all knew that the game was not won in the bus to the stadium, but instead between the white lines on the field.

As we went through warm-ups, I could sense that our drive, that was usually shared from player to player, was lower than it had been all season. From the onset, I sensed we were in trouble. Initially, I thought my emotions might have been a little premature, because CJ Spiller raced down the sideline during the opening kick-off for an 88-yard return for a touchdown. Maybe, my worst fears would not be realized, and many of our players were not in Tampa Bay already after all. The score gave us a quick lead, and let the air out of the roaring South Carolina faithful. I felt a boost of adrenaline rush through my body, and the defensive intensity was set as Coach Steele gave us our final instructions of the game plan.

South Carolina would score on their first drive, and again on their following drive. It was a typical rivalry game, and the Gamecocks played relentless football. They were playing us tough, as they did not have much to lose. They were not playing in the SEC championship game. Their head coach, Steve Spurrier, was their lead play caller and was known for being a mastermind with trick plays from his many years of coaching at Florida. This fact would hold true in this game as well, as he put his starting cornerback, Stephan Gilmore, in at quarterback, and ran a Tim Tebow Wildcat type of offense. We had practiced all week for this possibility. But no matter how many times you have practiced it against the scout team, it is nothing like the full speed action of a live game. At the half, South Carolina led 17-7, with big momentum on their side in front of their home crowd. During the second half of the game, we faltered and it seemed as if we could not buy a point. Turnovers hurt us, and gave South Carolina great field position. The Gamecock offense, through our faults, had short fields to work with. Add to that the inability of our defense to make stops, and it became ugly. We all failed to do what we were capable of that night. The result was a slow, painful loss to our rival. The final score read: South Carolina 34 – Clemson 17.

Despite the tough loss at South Carolina, we had to regroup fast. We had to prepare to play for the ACC Championship, which would be held in Tampa, Florida the following week. There was no time for regret and, even though we had lost the game to South Carolina, the buzz on campus was crazy. There was a refreshing vibe the entire week of preparation. We were back to business, and this was the team I knew; the one who had battled back and survived a slow start -- the team that was vying for the ACC Championship.

On Friday, we loaded the planes to the sound of cheers from our devoted fans. We all had one mission in mind, to bring that ACC Championship Trophy back to Clemson. I did not enjoy the flight to Tampa. It consisted of tossing and turning, and a lot of turbulence. I was sick to my stomach as we arrived at the Tampa International Airport. As the doors of the plane were opened, I walked down the stairs of the plane. I was thankful to God to have escaped the cold winter weather in the Carolinas, to enjoy a sunny, breezy day in Tampa, Florida. It was like returning home to the hot temperatures of South Alabama.

After securing our belongings, we would head over to Raymond James Stadium, which was not far from the Marriott Hotel where we were to stay, to get a look at the venue where we would be playing the next day. By the time we arrived at the stadium, it was raining heavily, but we were able to view the huge stadium from under the garage where our busses were parked. There were lots of people standing around the venue. The first thing I looked to see was the ship in the end zone. I had always wanted to see how they got a ship back there. From my vantage point, I saw the red steel constructed replica of a pirate ship in the back of the end zone, with a cannon ready to be fired every time the Bucs scored in a game. I always enjoyed playing at NFL stadiums for bowl games. These honors, Bowl Games, only came once a year. This time it was not just a bowl game; this was my first time playing in a game for the title.

After watching the rain muddy the field that we would play on the next day, we moved directly to the visitor locker room where we received a heartfelt motivational speech from our Head Coach, Dabo Swinney. His words had me ready to win. Afterwards, we departed the stadium in route to the Marriott. As we rode along heading to our hotel, I took pleasure in the beautiful view of Tampa Bay. One facility in particular caught my eye; Buccaneer One, the Tampa Bay Bucs Team Facility. As we passed it in the dark you could barely see it, but I imagined it to be a magnificent and magical place.

That night I had trouble sleeping. I was concerned about my parents, who were traveling to the game on the highways. I was also very excited to be playing in this game. My mind was working overtime, and my thoughts wandered. I thought of all of the pessimists in my life that said I would never make it out of the hood. I smiled, and I thought of those who said I would never make it to college. Here I was, and I had made it. Standing in the lovely, elegant Marriott Hotel, my mind was at peace, as I was preparing to start in the ACC Championship Game.

The next morning, I was the first player downstairs. I was ready to get to the stadium. I was in for a long wait at the hotel. We did not play until 8:00 pm that night. We went through a series of events: a pre-game breakfast, several meetings, and a pre-game meal before our final meeting as a defense.

In our final meeting, a crazy thing happened. Coach Steele was standing before the defensive players, speaking in the passionate voice that he always used with us, and suddenly just started screaming and shouting. "Tonight," Steele said, "men, we need to make them know that they are playing the best! We need to punish everyone who touches the ball!" We knew he was trying to motivate us, but this was highly out of character for him.

Things went south from there for Coach Steele, and later it would for us. In his attempt to get us focused, Coach Steele reared back with his arm and punched one of the steel chairs in the room hard, trying to make his point. This was the first time he ever did anything like that. As he continued talking, his face turned red and we could tell that he had hurt his hand. He was favoring it throughout the rest of his speech. He had broken his hand, and he collapsed from the pain. We were nervous about the predicament. Steele was not only our defensive caller, but he was the coach that signaled to us the best during the game.

I, and I am sure my other defensive teammates, wondered, "What are we going to do?" As we each exited the room toward the team busses, the doctors tended to Coach Steele.

Our hard-nosed Coach Steele was on the sideline later that night, with his hand heavily wrapped signaling. We found his strength amazing, even though the signaling of plays was a little different. Because Steele's hand was wrapped, the cornerback that was nearest our sideline relayed the call player-to-player, until it got to me. I signaled to the entire defense. It was a real adjustment, but I had played enough snaps to adjust to things on the fly.

The game was a typical Georgia Tech vs. Clemson battle. There was a lot of back-and-forth. The crowd seemed to be painted orange, as our fans traveled very well.

We had a special guest on our sideline, Mark Herzlich, a line- backer from Boston College. His presence added an extra level of inspiration to me. I was inspired by Mark's courage and level of commitment.

Mark, after his junior season, was regarded as a First Round Draft Pick. He decided to stay for his senior season. During his senior season, his life changed from fighting on the football field, to fighting a battle for his life, as he was diagnosed with a rare form of cancer in his leg. Cancer has always been my biggest fear. I felt that once you were diagnosed with cancer, you ultimately died. What I had learned throughout this season as I watched Mark battle back was that you can beat it with the secret ingredients of faith, heart, and dedication to win. I just stared at him as he smiled, watching the game. Mark had beaten cancer and he would return to the football field. He went on to win a Super Bowl with the Giants just two years later. What a story. Knowing his drive and seeing him on the sideline was inspiring not only to me, but the whole team.

The game was tough. There were highs and lows. The defense would have a big stop, and then Georgia Tech would have a big play. The field was muddy, which was tough because of the option attack. The conditions were especially difficult for me because I needed to be able to check the fake, or to get to the fullback, yet still be able to get back out for the quarterback if he kept the ball. One thing that was certain, CJ Spiller and the offense came to play. The offensive unit was scoring on nearly every drive. We dominated the opening quarter, controlling the game with a lead of 14-3. The second quarter, Georgia Tech came out with a couple of different plays in their option package offense, and led at halftime 16-13.

The message the coach gave us at halftime was simple. We had to stop giving up the big plays. Georgia Tech had scored several long touchdowns on busted assignments. The halftime break rejuvenated us, as we jogged out of the locker room and back to our sideline. After the half, it was starting to rain a little. We did not need anything else working against us, as we were already in a dogfight. We were down, with no answer for their option attack. Georgia Tech struck first after the half, with a run from their running back, Dwyer, but we quickly struck back with a 36-yard run from CJ Spiller.

I was on the sideline trying to get our guys going by saying, "Let's go baby! It is going to be on us to close this out at the end of the day! Trust me!"

I knew in my heart that my teammates were playing with everything in them. Nobody wanted to let any of the other teammates down. The following drive, we had them in a three in, three out situation, when we received a bad pass interference call. This sparked new life in Georgia Tech. They took advantage of it, too. Nesbitt play faked to the running back and threw a long pass to a wide-open Demetrius Thomas, as our cornerback slipped and fell on the wet ground. My heart dropped, as it reminded me of what happened in 2008 between the same two players. The pass seemed to spiral through the air forever.

I prayed silently, "Please, drop it. Please drop it."

Thomas did not even flinch as he caught the pass and sprinted down the sideline. The Georgia Tech fans and the crowd went crazy. The catch was a final deathblow in a game that I will never forget. We walked off the field, dodging the oranges that were being thrown at us from the stands by their rude fans. They were rubbing their victory in our faces. They were reminding us that Georgia Tech was heading to the BCS Orange Bowl game.

We got in so late that on the next morning, I overslept and missed church service. I was emotionally and physically exhausted. The feeling was similar to that of one mourning the loss of someone close. I realized that it was only a game, yet to lose in the form and fashion we lost, left a mark on me. I decided to use that chip on my shoulder as motivation to drive me in my preparation for the next season. I never wanted this feeling again. When things went wrong or something did not come out right in my life, I would try to find something positive in this experience to focus on. As I lay in my bed bruised, beaten, and battered by the physical play of the game, I took solace in the fact I would be able to integrate what I had learned this season into my life, and I used the experience to give the others a different perspective on the situation. I was taught that what matters most is not how things started for you but how you decide the end result. I would channel those thoughts heading into my junior year. I would apply them to my life, on the field and in the classroom.

We always seem to find time to have fun.
Fall Camp 2008 picture day
Left to right: Marcus Gilchrist, Sadat Chambers,
Chris Chancellor, DeAndre McDaniel.

My family was excited as I was at my first
career start vs Alabama 2008.

Moments I cherish.

Talking trash to Florida State quarterback, Christian Ponder, as he makes his checks in 2009.

By far the biggest linemen I had ever got a sack on vs TCU.

9

BECOMING A SERVANT

"For we are God's handiwork, created in Christ Jesus to do good works, which God prepared in advance for us to do."

Ephesians 2:10

I had learned a lot by observing Coach Swinney. Whenever he had an opportunity, he always made sure he gave back to the community. This was inspirational to me. It gave me a different perspective on being a servant. As my personal fame grew and my stage widened, I did not want to let an opportunity to give back to people pass me by, especially young people. I wanted to use what fame I had to impact young lives in a positive manner. I responded quickly to the requests of four people. These people were Jeff Davis, Amy Carpenter, Daniel Hall, and Scott Carpenter. Each provided me with an opportunity to serve youth in some way. Each also led me into some of the toughest schools and neighborhoods in South Carolina. These service projects inspired me to do more. I visited classrooms, both regular and those for the mentally challenged. I visited kids in the hospital. I did not care where I was sent. I just wanted to use my small piece of celebrity to bless the lives of others. I went into the service projects with the belief that I could provide hope and inspiration to young people, but I'm the one who came out blessed beyond measure. Most of the visits were financed out of my own pocket, and this was initially challenging. But when I thought of what a visit like this would have meant to me as a young person, it made me press on. I had come from humble beginnings, and I wanted to leave a legacy. This was the best way I knew how. Subsequently, the children and adults I encountered became more of an inspiration to me than I was to them.

The first person I reached out to was Jeff Davis. Jeff knows everyone around Clemson. He is dependable and trustworthy. I knew that if he could not help me with something, he would be able to point me in the right direction. Jeff is only about 6'1" in height, but he has a presence of someone much larger. Everyone respects him because he is a person of great integrity, and in spite of his many accomplishments, he is still very humble. Jeff was inducted into Clemson's Ring of Honor, and his name hangs on a Stadium banner. He was also a member of the 1981 National Championship team at Clemson University, and a member of the college football Hall of Fame. Many people know him as "The Judge." I knew right away if anyone could get me started in community service around Clemson, it was Jeff. Jeff understood me, and where I had come from. With his guidance, I had grown from being a hot-tempered freshman to a humble, mild-mannered citizen. I will take the lessons that he shared with me forever.

I remember my first encounter with Jeff Davis vividly. It occurred on my official visit to Clemson. I recognized him from all the pictures that hung in the athletic facilities.

I walked up to him, shook his hand, and as he was about to introduce himself, I said, "I am going to break all of your records."

He and I still laugh about that introduction. Though I did not break all of his records, I got close to a few during my career at Clemson. Jeff put me in contact with some of the schools in the area, where I would be able to go and read to the children. Serving in this capacity was definitely a sacrifice on my part. Time was already a precious commodity, but it was worth the sacrifice. I had to schedule the sessions between classes, studying film, and practices. Reading to the children in the morning meant that I had to get out of bed two or three hours earlier than everyone else. Serving as a reader to the children was tough, but God always provided me with the strength to make it through the rest of my day. The smiles on the kids' faces at the schools were so refreshing. I appreciated just being allowed to come in for that single hour. There were children that reminded me a lot of home. Many came from poverty like me, and seeing them smile as I read to them brought joy to my heart.

I continued to serve by reading at schools for months, before I decided to challenge myself. I wanted to see if this was just about fame and publicity for me. I did not want it to be. My desire was to serve God, through serving his children. Reading was great, yet I wanted to make a real sacrifice and step outside of my comfort zone. I began by reaching out to other people in the schools outside of Clemson for opportunities. Going outside of Clemson would require me to make sacrifices of not only time, but financial sacrifices as well. I have to admit I was concerned with this because I had a full load of classes, tutoring, film study, meetings, and practices to balance. I also would have to use my refund check to pay for the gas needed to travel. But God was faithful, and God provided everything I needed.

During my time at Clemson, I met two young boys named Will and Jack. I grew to love them as I would have loved two little brothers. They would hang over the walls as the team would walk into the locker rooms after games. They were always asking for things like gloves, wristbands, and even the tape from around your wrist. They made you feel like a star. Because of their enthusiasm and love for Clemson football, I asked Mike Hamlin to introduce me to them so that I could give the boys my gloves. I enjoyed spending time with them very much, and it became routine for me to meet them after the games to give them something. Over time, we developed a deep friendship. Through our interaction, I learned that the boys attended Taylors Elementary School and their mother, Amy, worked there as a third grade teacher. Taylors Elementary School was about 45 minutes away from Clemson, in Greenville. Their friendship meant a lot to me, so I would visit their elementary school frequently. I would attend school functions and speak to the students. I really loved this experience, and giving back to the community was very important to me. I wanted to use what I had learned to teach others, and to be a role model.

During my red-shirt junior season, I attended the Carnival at Taylors Elementary School. Tajh Boyd, a highly recruited freshman quarterback from Virginia, attended the Carnival with me.

Tajh and I had been friends before he came to Clemson University, because I had reached out to him through Facebook. When I first made contact with him, he was getting ready to play in the United States Army All-Star game. I respected him as a player, and I watched many of his highlight clips on Rivals Recruiting Website, and thought he could provide our offense with a boost in the future. He had a Michael Vick style of play. I believed that the versatility he possessed was something our team was missing at the quarterback position. Initially, he declined multiple friend requests from me, but I thought highly of him as a player, and sent him encouraging messages. One day he finally wrote me back. Eventually, I introduced him to Coach Swinney, and the rest is history.

The Carnival was fun. There, Tajh and I walked around dressed in our orange game day jerseys. I had been asked to sit in the dunking booth. I was asked to sit on a tiny seat, over a pool of water, as students threw a ball at a target, in attempts to put me in the water.

My intent was to serve, and I strongly believed in giving back, but getting wet was not part of the plan. In the interest of safety, and of staying dry, I declined the dunking booth. Instead, I served in another capacity wisely. I signed autographs and tossed the football with young boys. When I tossed the ball back and forth to the children, I thought of my childhood. I remembered my uncle Doug. I saw myself in the eyes of these children, who were so excited about catching the football. Their excitement and eagerness inspired me. I understood that I was once in the exact same position they were in, and perhaps, one may have the same dreams that I had as a boy. Through giving to others, God opened my eyes to see how special the simple gift of service was. On the ride back to Clemson after the Carnival, I listened to Tajh talk about how much attending the Carnival had impacted him. He said that no matter how much fame he attained, that giving back to the community would always be a priority in his life. I was very blessed that, through my service, I had shared a blessing with my friend. Becoming a servant is its own reward.

After visiting Taylor Elementary, word quickly spread through the media that I was out in the community and giving back.

My next service opportunity came by way of an invitation from Scott. Scott called and asked if I would go to his daughter's school and speak to her class. His daughter, Meg, attended Plain Elementary, which is also in the Greenville area. I quickly accepted the offer; not realizing then that one of the students would become an inspiration to me. The visit occurred on a morning that nothing seemed to line up right for me. It was a cold morning, and I had to wake at about 6 AM. Getting out of bed was a struggle, and I did not want to get out from under my warm, cozy comforter. It was still dark outside, and I thought of reconsidering this request. I toyed with the idea of calling Scott to cancel, but I could not. I knew how much my being there meant to the kids. It is funny how much the devil will fight you when you are on the verge of a blessing.

I had an 11 o'clock class that day, and grabbed my books because I would not have time to get them after speaking. When I was prepared to walk out of the door, I could not find my keys. The search for the keys took about thirty minutes. As I got in the car, I sighed with discontentment. It started to rain. The tires on my car were worn and struggled to find traction, as water began to build up on the highways. I continued with a bit of fear in my heart.

I spoke to God in prayer saying, *"Lord, you know my heart and I know how big this is for the kids. Protect me and let me reach this school safely. Amen."*

My relationship with God during this time was strong, and I had faith that whenever I was in trouble, God was close. God showed up on time and my faith in Him increased. Almost immediately after praying, it stopped raining. The storm ceased, and a bright sun appeared miraculously. Before long I was arriving at my destination. There was a newly built brick building in front of me with a sign that read Plain Elementary. I thanked God for answering my prayer. Scott and his brother who was a local photographer accompanied me. We went to the front office first to check in and the teacher of the class, Mrs. Oliver, greeted us. Everyone in the front office including the principal, Debbie Mihalic, was very polite.

"Brandon Maye, you are truly a class act!" the principal proclaimed.

I was simply humbled. I thanked them for thinking so highly of me and for trusting me to speak with their children. I did not take these types of opportunities lightly. I counted each endeavor as a blessing. The students welcomed me like royalty. Classes flooded the hallways clapping and many of the students were wearing Clemson-orange shirts in my honor. I also took note of the couple of USC Gamecocks shirts within the crowd. We were, after all, in South Carolina. I remember how attentive the students were as I stressed the importance of education. I told the story that Coach Bowden shared with me, specifically for the young boys in the crowd who had dreams of playing in the NFL. I wanted them to understand how important getting an education was, and I emphasized that only a small percentage of players make it to the pros. My goal was not to destroy the dreams of these young people. I simply wanted to help them comprehend the fact that football could be taken away, but education could not. My speech lasted for about 45 minutes. My humble prayer was that I was able to touch one child that day. I think that was achieved. I hung around for an extra 30 minutes to sign autographs and answer questions. I made a mental note of one special autograph request. This was the first time someone wearing a South Carolina shirt asked me, a Clemson player, for an autograph. I imagined the grief this little fellow would get when he got home, but indulged his request. I felt sorry for that kid. I would have liked to be a fly on the wall when he got home to his family.

While I was signing autographs, Ms. Lanie begged me to speak to her class. Ms. Lanie is one of Amy's best friends, and a good friend to me. Ms. Lanie is a special education teacher. I was at a loss for words. As I made my way towards her classroom, I began stressing over what to say. I did not have any idea what I had gotten myself into. Blindly, I thought that her students were experiencing things in life that I could not relate to. I was wrong, and spending time with her students inspired me. I remember entering a room full of excited children. I remember lots of hugs. I will always cherish having my picture taken with a beautiful, blonde, blind girl. I was in front of the class, as the teachers grabbed her hand to lead her to me. I suggested that I come to her instead.

When she heard me, she quickly replied, "I am fine. I am walking to you."

I almost burst into tears when she walked towards me. I was

amazed by her strength and courage. She did not use her blindness as an excuse or allow me to pity her. When she was close to me, I wrapped my arms around her, posed, and smiled for the picture. I learned not to take things for granted from this little girl. Her calm strength and faith touched me, and I felt a connection to her spirit. This was only the beginning. As I made my way around the room, I could see out of the corner of my eye Ms. Lanie standing with this dark skinned, neatly dressed girl that looked to be about 6 years old. She was tugging, pulling and trying to get to me, to introduce herself. Ms. Lanie was working hard to hold her back, as I finished taking pictures with some of the other kids in the class. I finished and, when I turned towards Ms. Lanie and the little girl, I was met with a big, warm hug.

"You got big muscles," she shouted.

I laughed out loud and kept smiling. Ms. Lanie stood just beside us.

"Brandon, this is Treasure. She is in love with Brandon Maye," Ms. Lanie said. Treasure jumped back into the conversation, "You play football. I want you to be my boyfriend."

Everyone in the classroom was laughing at this point. Treasure stole my heart, and I did not mind at all. She made me feel like I was the biggest celebrity in the world. In her eyes there was nothing better than me, Brandon Maye. I left the classroom more inspired than ever. I thought the students would be uncooperative or problematic, but they touched my heart and taught me something through my interaction with them. The class left me speechless. That night Ms. Lanie called me and told me how thankful she was for me coming to visit her class.

She told me that the students raved over me all day, especially Treasure, saying, "Brandon Maye, this. Brandon Maye, that."

Despite a rough start, the day turned out great. And if I had canceled, I would have missed out on this wonderful blessing. Isn't that just like God? I explained to Ms. Lanie that her students made a huge impact on my life.

She and Amy got the boys and Treasure together, and we met for dinner the next week in Easley, South Carolina. Treasure was just as excited as she was the first time she saw me in the classroom. I made a promise to her that if I ever have a baby girl, that I would name her Treasure. Her energy and passion were mind-boggling. I found it hard to believe that a simple visit to someone's school meant so much.

There was one element of service missing in my experiences. I had not ventured into the environments that were similar to where I grew up. Most of my service thus far was in nice areas or gated communities. I wanted very much to influence and make an impact on "my own." I wanted to talk to those types of kids, and show them that no matter the hand you are dealt, you can make it. They could use me as an example. Most of the kids needed to see there was hope, and I was an example of that hope. I wanted them to understand that if you had God in your life, anything was possible. The only thing that could limit you was you yourself. And if you work hard enough, you could be great. I did not know of any of those areas near Clemson that would provide me with the opportunity to minister to those children who grew up so much like me.

That was when I thought of my spiritual 2-a-day mentor, Daniel Hall. Daniel was the assistant principal at Lakeside in Anderson, South Carolina. Anderson was a small town about 20 minutes from Clemson. All the things I survived growing up were present in some manner in Anderson-violence, drugs, and disrespectful kids. I remembered many conversations I had with Daniel, when he told me of having to suspend a student for fighting or getting into an argument with a teacher. In some cases he told me some of the students were arrested. Daniel was one of those principals that hated to take disciplinary actions towards the kids, and you could hear the concern in his voice. He built a tight bond with many of the boys, bringing them to our practices and fan day events just trying to let them see things from a positive view. Most of the kids lived in similar areas like I had growing up, surrounded by poverty. The only difference was that most of them did not have the same support I had growing up. They were not taught the simple things like yes sir and yes ma'am. I talked to Daniel and told him I wanted to come to his school and he set it up.

One morning my teammate, Miguel Chavis, and I headed over to Anderson to speak to the boys at Mr. Hall's school. Mr. Hall organized our session into two different speaking events, as the young men at the school were evenly divided into groups. Each group consisted of about 40 young males. All of those young men were looking for a person to follow. They were at that stage in life where they were looking for a role model, whether negative or positive. I remember Mr. Hall telling me that most of the boys were heavy into gang banging. With that understanding, my approach to that day was to strip myself of any pride that may have been in my body. I actually wanted to get down to their level, sharing stories that they could relate to. At some point in my life, I had experienced everything that those boys were experiencing now. Those kids locked on to my message, of making choices, and the value of education. We stood in the middle of the library, wearing our purple team jerseys. I knew that there was no way we could change the situation for every single boy in that room, but if we reach just one, I think God's will was done. This was the first time I had seen myself as a child again. I saw myself reflected in the eyes of those young men, as they looked up at me. I could see the pain of poverty, no hope, and only a dream that seems so far away.

I said to myself as we exited the front entrance of the school and got into the car to go to football practice at Clemson, "at one time, that was me."

I will always remember that day and thank God for the opportunity to be able to speak to those children, and I pray we made a difference in just one life.

After those initial events, the opportunity to give back continued to present itself. I became very active in the holiday canned food drive that was held through the Salvation Army. Those experiences were very humbling, of handing food out to those who were needy. There were events where moms would come with 5 kids, and you could see the hunger on their faces. At these events, I had a chance to put the strength that I had built up through working out to good use. I helped unload trucks, with large brown boxes that were full of food: a frozen turkey, snacks, sandwich meat, and frozen meals. I had lived though poverty in a sense, but my mom worked extremely hard, using her disability check to make sure that my sisters and I wanted for nothing we needed. This experience made me more grateful for what I went through in my childhood. Though we did not have much, seeing those hungry kids, I was very thankful that we never went hungry.

Every year, Clemson held the Special Olympics where the track team would compete. We were usually presented with the option to participate or not, but it was on Saturdays, and most players used it as their rest day. I looked at it as another opportunity to pay God back for getting me out of the hood, and getting a scholarship so that I could attend college. If you were not humble and grounded before you went to see these kids compete, after you left the Special Olympics you were. You also went away encouraged because you saw so many that could have thrown in the towel, and said I am special. They could have just given up on life. Even though I found attending challenging because it was always so hot, those participants never complained. I always enjoyed watching them compete, despite their circumstances, for that day they enjoyed just being normal.

The reason I give back and worked hard in the community was to inspire, as I was a living witness that, no matter how hard things get, you can still reach greatness. It never failed, when I went out in the South Carolina communities that I would go there with a mind-set to show people that, if you put your mind to something, you can achieve it. I always went with the intention of motivating them, but the groups always ended up motivating me.

Enjoyed Plain Elementary. The smiles on these babies faces at 8am was priceless.

Visit to Dodge Elementary.

Treasure. I spoke at her school one morning and she ended up inspiring me more than I could ever inspire her. The teachers got her parents permission and I met them for dinner.

Having fun with the amazing hall animations at Plain Elementary.

This little girl doesn't know how much she made my day to see her smiling. She was blind, but instead of feeling down she's smiling.

Teaming up with Cobi Ham of Arkansas inspiring the youth.

10

JOB-LIKE FAITH

"Count it all joy, my brothers, whenever you face trials of many kinds."

James 1:2. NIV

"Wow!" is what I thought to myself the entire summer, heading into the 2010 Fall Term.

It seemed unreal to me that I was about to enter my senior semester in the classroom, and my red-shirt junior year on the football field. It seemed like only yesterday that I sat in the back seat of that rental car, as my parents drop me off for Freshman Report Day. I remember lying in the back seat, with a towel over my face, having many of the same thoughts that any freshman would have when leaving home for college for the first time. I remember how uncertain I had felt. Throughout my first three years of college, I had survived many ups and downs. I am thankful that that uncertainty was quickly replaced with joy, hope, and a personal relationship with Christ. Going through the demands of being a student-athlete in a Division I football program was difficult, but God was with me all the time. I was now a firm believer in the scripture 1 Corinthians 10:13, that God would never put on us more than we could bear. I had endured with faith and hope in God, and he was working everything out for my good. As I entered into this year, I consider myself now more than ever, a living testimony. God had truly placed his hand on my life, and had made my life be where he would get the glory.

Up to this point, my success on the football field had been stellar. I had accumulated almost 200 career tackles, one interception, 12 tackles for loss, and broke the Clemson team record for forced fumbles in a season. Through all the successes, I remained the same person that I had been during those lonely years of my childhood. I did not read the newspaper clippings, or even notice my statistics, but the NFL scouts did.

During that summer, I thought often about how things would be if I had a great junior season on the football field. If things went well, I could possibly be in a situation where I would have to decide whether to enter the NFL draft at the end of my junior year, or return to Clemson for my senior year. The whole time, I thought about how I could be a blessing to my family that had struggled at times financially. I remember the promise that I made to my mom, that if I succeeded, she would never have to work again. Those thoughts were driving me in my workouts, my eating habits, and on team runs. I had seen players that had high round NFL draft grades leave early. I knew my mom was not really a fan of those types of decisions.

She often instructed me, "You need to get that education."

I was young at the time, so I would reply, "Mama, if I left early and signed for 10 million dollars, I would not need the education."

I know without a doubt that the comment I made as a youngster was foolish. I know that education is the key to many avenues in life. I also know that money cannot buy happiness, or a ticket into heaven. And I also knew that I would be a hypocrite, because I had told so many young people that education was the key to success.

During the previous year, 2009, I had experienced not only success on the football field, but success in the classroom as well. I held many leadership roles around the Clemson campus. I had been name to the All-ACC Academic Team for the second time, and I was looking for a 3-peat this season. I was selected to be a leader and I understood that the job of a leader is to serve others. I was only one of three football players selected to be part of the Student-Athlete Advisory Committee. Our objective was to be a spokesperson for the football team. Most of the assignment centered on the athletes per forming community service, and I loved giving back.

Amidst all the good things that I had going for me in my life at the time, I was not prepared for the storm that was coming. The storm came in the form of disappointments and tragedies. Despite reaching the goals I had set for myself, spiritually I was being tested in many areas. In spite of this, I held close to my relationship with God. This year would really test my faith, and allow me to see how far I had come spiritually in my walk with the Lord. I was mindful that things could turn sour quickly. I would attend the regular Bible study services at New Holy Light Church in Pendleton. When I look back on it now, I realize this was a huge part of the refining process in my life, taking me from that rough stone to a faceted diamond. This season in my life was huge in the diamond cutting process. As painful as it was, I know I had to go through it and it only increased my faith in God.

After losing to Georgia Tech in the ACC Championship Game, our team went to play at the Music City Bowl. I still wasn't over the disappointment of how my sophomore season had ended. During the game against Kentucky, I injured my foot on the first play. Consequently, I missed the rest of the game. It marked the first time in my college career that I had to stand on the sidelines and watch my team play. Sadly, it would not be the last time.

As the team entered into spring training, Kevin Steele approached me. He informed me that he was moving me to a new position, outside linebacker. This news was shocking because I had played middle linebacker throughout my entire college career. I understood that my teammate, Kavell Conner, was drafted, and now started as a linebacker for the Indianapolis Colts, but I was truly disappointed at this decision by my coach. I really did not understand it, especially during this crucial point in my career, but I trusted his decision. I was the leading tackler on the team in the previous season, going into the bowl game. I thought to myself, this was nothing but the devil. To make matters worse not only was I moved to another position, I was listed as a co-starter. The media tried hard during interviews to try to get me to say something bad about the coaches. While I responded honestly to the questions, I did not let them know how disappointed I was.

I stated boldly, "my job is to perform, and I let the coaches take care of the decision making. At the end of the day, the cream would rise to the top."

The position switch required me to do some things that I was not use to doing. For example, skill-wise I had to learn covering. I gladly accepted this challenge. I wondered if the new coaching staff was having the same thoughts as those other college recruiters who did not think I was good enough to play Division 1 football. The spring practices were a humbling experience for me. I mainly played with the second team, as Jonathan "Tig" Willard, a redshirted freshman, received most of the snaps with the first unit.

I have never been the type to worry about another player and their skill levels; I had always been confident that I was the best. Though cognizant of the changes, I continued to tell myself that "The cream is going to rise to the top," over and over again when I found myself upset. I may have had a long face sometimes, but the coaches did not know they had added fuel to my fire. When the Spring Practices came to an end, I had adjusted to my new position well. I went back and forth on whether to go talk to Coach Steele. I decided to accept this situation as a challenge. I respected my coaches' decisions, and owed respect to my teammates as well. I had faced challenges before, and positioned myself to handle the business at hand in an appropriate manner. This was merely another test, and I had to apply all that I had learned in life to pass it.

During summer workouts, I still trained and motivated my teammates as before. Being a leader was never an act to me, I was born for this. Even though I was on the second team at the time, I used it as an opportunity to lead the group that was out there with me when we would go through player-run skills and drills. These drills were vital times for team success, as we ran all the drills without any coaches. Most of the players that were on the second team with me were freshman and sophomores. I took this as an opportunity to help and try to teach them the game. They usually had limited game experiences, if any. I had played in some big time games, and my knowledge could lead to them having successful careers. If I would have wallowed in self-pity or gotten mad about the position change, I would have missed out on the opportunity to once again serve.

When fall camp came around, I was quite familiar with the outside linebacker position that the coaches had switched me to. I decided that I would do all I could to make the best of the situation, and I took it upon myself to learn the plays and get in the film room. I would control those things I could control. My preparation was evident, as I dominated in camp. Scrimmage after scrimmage, I was graded highest of all the linebackers. During camp, I was eventually penciled in at the starting outside linebacker position. This came after working countless hours to learn the position. The situation made me reflect on my childhood. I recalled the numerous times when my back had been against the wall, and the perception that I was destined for failure. I did not accept failure. I acknowledged the fact that I always had a choice. If I would have quit initially when Coach Steele informed me about the move, I would had never learned this lesson. I would have missed out on how adjusting to change relates to life.

As the end of Fall Camp was approaching, I realized that personally I had accomplished the best camp of my career. I was spiritually, mentally, and physically ready to have another amazing season. Camp concluded in early September 2010, the week before we played our season opener. The season-opener would be played at home against North Texas. I was excited and called my mom to share the good news with her.

I remember saying, "I had my best camp ever. This season is going to be remarkable. I am going to win the Butkus."

I was raring to go, and the statements I made to my mother were reinforced by Coach Swinney. I appreciated his candor as he expressed what I felt inside during a pre-season interview.

"Brandon just finished the best camp of his career," Swinney said.

On Thursday of that week, before the first game, everything changed. I started to feel some major pain in my right knee. When I would bend the knee or run, there was a popping, clicking sensation. I tried to ignore it, and chalked it up as nothing major. I had always played the tough guy, and continued to go on as normally as possible. I just thought that the pain was some of the normal aches and pains that came from playing football. I had started for

26 games straight, so I just simply disregarded it. After practice, I just went to my apartment without visiting the training room. I had dealt with the training staff since I had been in high school, and I understood the process.

"Put some ice on it," I often joked with my teammates about how much the trainers used ice. I would say, "If your heart stopped beating, the trainers would just inform their assistants to put some ice on it, and it would start beating again."

My plan was to do just that, put some ice on it and elevate it once I got inside my apartment. The parking lot was quiet and dark. As I started to get out of the car, I reached across the passenger seat to grab my book bag. As I started to roll my body out from under the steering well, I placed my left foot onto the ground. Once my left foot was set firmly, I began to push myself up from my low-seated Dodge charger. Then, I brought my right leg around to get out. That was when I knew something was not quite right. My knee felt extremely heavy, and the pain was more intense. There was a violent popping sound. Again, I just tried to minimize it.

The next morning, I woke up to find my knee puffy and very inflamed. This was the first time I really became worried about it. I rushed to the training room to see Danny Poole, the head trainer. I wanted his staff to take a look at it.

The whole drive from my apartment to the training room, I prayed to myself, "Please Lord... Please don't let this be anything major. You know how hard I have worked for this upcoming season. Give me favor."

After an MRI, my worst fears were confirmed, and I got the news that I did not want to hear. I had to have arthroscopic surgery on my knee to remove a loose body that was causing the swelling and popping. The prognosis was a devastating blow to me initially, but there was some good news. If I rehabilitated well, and worked hard, I could return for the third game of the season. That game would be against Auburn University. My only concern was how quickly I could rehabilitate my knee, and how my performance would be affected. I knew that I had won the starting position, but I believe the coaches would move me back to the second team because of the prognosis. It was all in God's and Coach Swinney's hands. Fortunately for me, God gave me favor. Also, Coach Swinney had a firm philosophy that nobody could lose a position due to injury. The decision was made for me to have surgery now, though it was not what I wanted. Surgery would force me to miss the first two games of the season against North Texas, and Presbyterian College.

The first two weeks of the 2010 season were tough for me. I was on the sidelines, with a jersey on watching my teammates play. Although I supported my teammates, I wanted to actively participate. Being reduced to a cheerleader created a hunger inside me, and motivated me to get back on the field. I put in countless hours of rehabilitation on my knee. I was driven. I knew that the first two games would be warm-ups for tougher opponents. I needed to be ready when my opportunity came again. The team was successful without my contribution, as Clemson completely outmatched both opponents, winning in flawless fashion.

After the Presbyterian game, I returned to the practice field. I was allowed to do some light work on Monday, as the trainers were trying to ease me back into the flow of things. We had a huge test waiting for us. This week we would be competing on "The Plains". We were preparing to play at Auburn University. My mindset was focused and determined. I yearned for not only an opportunity to play again, but also the opportunity to show my coaches that I was ready to contribute in a major way. Towards the middle of the week, my prayers were answered as I was put back with the starting unit.

I was only at about 70%, but I did not show any limp or signs of pain. The only mechanism I had problems concealing was stopping and starting when initiating lateral movements. I must have disguised it well because the coaches did not notice. It even surprised me when no one asked about it.

We made our way to Auburn University that Friday. It felt great to be back with my teammates, especially after the long hours isolated in the training room, completing rehabilitation while they were on the field. I was both thrilled and agitated. The ride to Auburn University was long and painful. My knee was uncomfortable and as a result, it stiffened. After about five hours of riding, I was excited even more when we finally arrived at Auburn University. I really hate road trips like this one to Auburn, sites where the coaches consider the venue close enough for us to drive.

That game had really been promoted heavily by ESPN. It was going to be a prime time, night game. Recently, the SEC had signed a contract with ESPN, and we always heard that the SEC was considered the toughest conference in college football. Auburn had recently signed Cam Newton, a huge commitment from a junior college. Within his first two games, he started to catch the eyes of many coaches. Our coaches were no exception. Throughout the entire week, all they talked about was, "Stop Cam Newton!" After watching his film all week, it was easy to see that Cam Newton was the real deal.

I was also reminded that Auburn and Alabama had passed on me during my high school recruiting season, so I was glad that I would have a chance to play both teams. It was also close to my family, so many would be able to attend. Because of all of these factors, there was extra motivation for me to perform well that particular night.

We had a great game plan, and initially it worked. We began the game dominating Auburn 17-3. I remember playing sparingly throughout the game, as this was my first live-action play since the knee surgery. During the second half, Auburn changed their game plan and came out of the locker room with a renewed vigor.

I believe someone must have said, "Let #2 take over!" referring to Cam Newton.

Our Clemson Defense made Auburn's superstar work for every pass that he completed. And if he tried to run, there was a price to pay. Trying to stop Cam Newton made this one of the most physical games I had ever played in. Several players were carted off the field. After the half, our domination of Auburn stopped and they were able to create momentum off of our turnovers. Auburn made a comeback and sent the game into overtime, with a score of 24-24. We ended up losing the game to Auburn. It was a heartbreaking loss. The game ended under bizarre circumstances. Our kicker actually made a field goal to send the game into a second overtime. There was a penalty or something. The referee waved it over. Our kicker attempted again, and missed on the second field goal attempt. I found out later that the call by the official was actually made from video evidence. But that is the world of college football. All I think of now, aside from the loss, is how I felt after. It was difficult for me to get a feel for how my outside linebacker position worked. It was very challenging. I remember running on and off the field in response to the sub packages we had put in for this game, to try to stop Cam Newton. I also remember a play that happened earlier in the game when my helmet got pulled off by a lineman. I remember it fondly because I made a tackle on Auburn's running back, Michael Dyer, with no helmet on. My dreads were swinging side-to-side, and it felt good.

After the Auburn loss, we had a bye week. The timing of the bye week was perfect for me. Instead of going home, I decided to stay in Clemson to get more treatment on my knee. My desire was to get my knee back to 100% for the rest of the season. Our record was 2-1 at the bye week, and the next game on the schedule was the University of Miami.

The next game on the schedule was Miami, and I felt confident. I simply had fun on the field, and allowed God to use me. It was exhilarating to be completely healed. I was back, back to making plays and jumping around, celebrating with my teammates. Against Miami, I had a big game. I made 7 tackles and 2 tackles for losses, but we lost the game. Our defense gave up too many big plays, and our offense did not capitalize on the offensive side of the ball. At 2-2, our season was starting to turn in the wrong direction. I attributed our performance to the emotional loss to Auburn.

The season was not turning out right for me, or the team. My aspirations were to excel in the classroom and on the football field, be a contributing part of a Clemson National Championship, and leave early for the NFL. With two early losses on our record, the dream of the title was clearly out of the picture, so I adjusted my ambition. I figured out that I still had a chance to improve my performances. By improving myself individually, I would give the Clemson defense a boost, too.

The next week we traveled by bus to Chapel Hill to play North Carolina. North Carolina was always a challenge for us. They were well coached by Butch Davis, and had a tremendous amount of talent and depth on their team, especially on defense. One of the things I enjoyed, as much as beating a team in their home stadium, was touring the places we went to play. North Carolina was no exception. When I thought of North Carolina, I thought of Michael Jordan, and all of the great basketball players who played there. After walking around the locker room and looking into the stands at all of that Carolina Blue, I cleared my mind and refocused on the task at hand.

My knee was ready to be tested, and this UNC game would provide that assessment. I knew that I had earned, and would receive a significant amount of playing time. This game would be like a coming out party for me at the outside linebacker position. If a person did not know any better, one would have thought I had been playing that position for a long time. I played with a swagger that was hard to match, even in pass coverage. My mentor, Uncle Pearl, a Pastor out of Atlanta, Georgia, always reminded me to do everything with power and authority. He taught me to do everything for God's glory and the building of his kingdom. Those words revitalized me the whole game, as I tolerated a little pain from the knee surgery with such a quick come back. With my confidence and knee back, there was still one thing missing. Clemson was losing close games. We lost to North Carolina in the closing seconds, 21-16. The flat performance started with the Auburn game, continued through the Miami game, and was still prevalent for the North Carolina game. We, as a team, seemed lifeless and unresponsive to challenges, and as a result we in lost in the closing minutes of those games.

The next week in the game against Maryland, I suffered another injury. I pulled my calf muscle on the first possession of the game. This was another unfortunate situation. I had just survived a sophomore season of slumps, and now I was in a junior year slump. It was not easy. I spent a lot of lonely nights in my apartment. I drew strength from studying the book of Job. During this season, I saw to a large extent, a connection to what I was experiencing and the struggle and pain that Job had to endure. If you read from the book of Job, you may see what I saw. Satan had to ask God's permission to test his servant Job. God allowed Satan to test him by taking away the things he valued most, in an attempt to try and force Job to curse God during his suffering. Job passed his test, and was blessed even more in the end. In my life, I thought of it as God allowing Satan to test me. I was going through some hardships. Enduring my ordeals was difficult, but I would never curse God. I chose to keep praying and thanking God, the one who had given me all I had.

It was sincerely a tough, dismal season already. I was struggling as an individual, and Clemson was struggling as a football team. Tragedy struck next. As I already mentioned, there were troubles. The only thing that kept my mind settled and focused was reading my bible, constant communication with my family, intimate conversations with my girlfriend, and encouragement from my good friend, Aylsia Womack.

On Monday morning, the week of the Georgia Tech Game, I overslept. Mondays are always challenging for me. I am normally sore and my body was still in recovery-mode from the Saturday game. This particular morning, I found myself running late for class, and I scrambled around my apartment looking for my keys. I hated to be late for class. I found it hard to lead others when you were not prompt. I searched around my apartment for my keys for about 30 minutes, and finally found them under my bed. I rushed out of the door and headed towards campus. I had the strangest feeling inside. I was a bit melancholy, full of a sadness I could not explain. I knew that something bad was coming, but I could not for the life of me figure out what that something was. I fought the unhealthy thoughts, and went along with my schedule as normally as I could.

"The day will get better," I said to myself as I rode through campus.

When I finally saw Brackett Hall, where my Research Methods Class was held, I had to face the additional challenge of finding a parking spot. I waited patiently by the stop sign, knowing I was already late for class, but hoping someone's time was up on the meter. I got lucky. A lady walked to her car and pulled off. I quickly raced to get the now vacant parking spot. By this time, I was 30 minutes late for class. As I dropped coins into the parking meter, I thought over whether or not I should even go to class. Even though it was the last thing I wanted to do, I just went in late and told my professor what had happened. It was the right thing to do. I was not a repeat offender. I started my walk towards the building. When I was about

50 yards from the entrance door, my cell phone rang. I usually put my cell phone on silent-mode on my way to class, but in my rush to get there today I forgot.

Ring..ring.

I looked at my cell phone to see who was calling. It was my cousin Porsche. I was worried because she never called me this early on a weekday morning. Knowing I was already late for class, I just let the phone go to voicemail. Throughout the remainder of the class, the fact that Portia had called me so early continued to bother me. I thought to myself, "Call her back. Call her back. Something is wrong."

I paid no attention to that voice in my head until my cell phone rang again. It was Portia calling again.

I tried to shrug it off thinking, "She must miss me dearly or have something very important to tell me."

I did not ignore her call this time. I went ahead and answered. I said, "Hello, Portia! You must really miss me."

Without even saying good morning, she began talking rapidly.

She was crying and I could not understand what she was trying to tell me.

"Hold on!" I replied as I started to walk back outside.

I was hoping the pause would give her a chance to gather herself. "Okay I am back," I said. "What are you saying?"

I could hear her more clearly now, but what she said next made me wish that I hadn't.

In a soft, woeful voice she said, "Alysia died."

Upon hearing those words, I started to go through all the Alysia's I knew.

I asked, "Which one?" I think I was in shock. I asked again, Which one? My friend, Alysia?" I nearly dropped the phone. "Alysia Womack?" I asked again in a shaky voice.

Portia said, "Yes."

"Are you serious? I will call you right back", I said.

After hearing the news, I needed some time to myself. Slowly the initial shock was wearing off, and tears began to run down my face. Not only was Alysia my cousin, she was my best friend as well. I trusted her completely. She was somebody I could tell everything to, and she always had words of wisdom to give to me. During my time at Clemson, and specifically throughout this troublesome season, her encouraging words had been invaluable. Her words encouraged me to keep pressing towards the mark. She was a soft-spoken, wonderful person. She had a smile that would light up the room. I did not want to believe what I had heard.

"This cannot be!" I said.

I had just spoken to Alysia two days ago, and still had the text messages on my phone that she sent me every morning as encouragement. As the cold wind blew across my face, all I could think about was how she and my family were supposed to be coming up for the next game. Alysia was only 19 years old, much too young to die. During a routine exam, the doctors had found a cancerous tumor on her brain. They told her it was in the last stages. She had an appointment scheduled with the doctors to remove the tumor the next day, but God must have needed another angel, and in Alysia he had one. God's plan for Alysia had prevailed. I could picture her as one of God's angels going home to heaven. I thought about our last conversation; I had asked her what she was going to do for her birthday.

Losing Alysia was another tough blow for me. Losing her meant I lost my best friend in the world. It always amazes me how things can quickly change in your life. After all of the success I had attained and enjoyed during my first two years at Clemson, this season was proving to be the most difficult. And now, all of a sudden, I had lost my best friend too. This was one of the lowest points in my life, and I was in a perpetual state of confusion and unhappiness. I found myself unable to concentrate and I found myself doing with injury after injury. Through all of the turmoil, I learned that life is way too short, and that I should value everyday God allowed me to wake up. I learned to cherish each moment; it may be your last. Alysia's death revived my spirit. Even in death, she helped me to see things clearer, and gave me a new perspective on life.

The rest of the week was very difficult for me. As the team was preparing for Georgia Tech, I spent most of my time on the sidelines watching. Because of my injury, I practiced in a very limited capacity and I became concerned about how much playing time I would actually see during Saturday's game. I was torn between being there with my teammates competing, and going home to attend Alysia's funeral service. Coach Steele assured me that I was going to play in Saturday's game against Georgia Tech, so I decided to stay for the game. My heart was heavy during the whole week of preparation. I felt guilty about not attending Alysia's funeral service. And Saturday just added to my guilt. During the game, I did not play one snap. Afterwards, I was very bitter about this. I felt betrayed. I felt as if they had lied to me, and I should have been allowed to attend Alysia's funeral. Though the next week I was back on the field practicing, not being able to say goodbye to my best friend still hurt me. But I had to find a way to forgive my coach for the pain in my heart. I know that is what Alysia would have wanted. I will never forget my best friend.

Our record at this point in the season was 3 – 4, which was very disheartening. This was the first time since I had been a football player at Clemson that we were fighting to even attend a bowl game. This week, we would be traveling to play at Boston College. Throughout the entire week, I found my mind was distracted. I was still preoccupied with Alysia's death, and holding on to her memory. This would be the first opportunity I had to start in a game since her death. I made up my mind that I would play for her, and I would play my heart out. During the initial drive, I was constantly in the backfield. On the third possession, Coach Steele substituted me out of the game. I did not understand what was going on.

"Was this thing personal," I questioned to myself.

I thought I was playing well, and had just been taken out of the game for no apparent reason. For much of the game, I just sat on the sidelines and took what few snaps that were given to me that day. Sometimes I found it hard to keep my composure. The only thing that kept me going was remembering what I had been told by Coach Rumph. He always told us that no matter how many snaps you get, you make sure you leave your mark on that game. That Saturday I, indeed, left my mark on that cold day in Chestnut Hill. I had my first double digit tackle game, with 12 tackles and three for a loss. I was getting back into the groove of things, and I was ready to be a powerful force throughout the rest of the season. Unfortunately for Clemson, we lost 10 to 16. Throughout most of our games, we would falter and lost many close games. But that day, I wasn't really concerned about Clemson's record. My main goal had been to play for my new Angel, Alysia.

As a team, it was obvious we were searching for our identity at the wrong part of the season. The season was quickly coming to an end, and we had yet to find our rhythm. Instead of improving as a team, it seemed as if every player was looking around waiting for someone else to make a play. Our leadership was obviously not as strong as it had been in previous seasons. There were others who only led when it was convenient to do so. I guess I should explain what I mean by this. There were some players that would lead when it looked good for them, or when it was convenient, such as when the media or coaches were present. What our team was lacking was leadership off the field too. This was in sharp contrast to the leadership we had during 2009, with players like Thomas Austin and Michael Palmer. Those were the guys who worked hard, regardless of who was present. Those guys did not settle for anything less than everyone's best. Because of their leadership, we had played for the title.

Surprisingly, after the loss to Boston College, the team played as a whole the next week during our game against NC State. We fought, and finally won a very close game. The score might not have been pretty, but the win kept us alive to play in a bowl game. Playing in the NC State game was the most fun I had had in a game all season because we were working so well together. Everyone was clicking. There was an excitement in the air, and a huge crowd. One would have thought that with our record, the fans would have bailed on us. But not the Clemson faithful, they showed out to support us rain or shine. We had fans that believed in us, and showed their support throughout this difficult season. That is what made Clemson such a special place.

The NC State game was to be played at noon. Early games gave me time to spend with my family at my apartment. During that game, we were playing in front of a huge crowd, but that was nothing compared to knowing my family was in the stands. They were waiting for me outside, so I rushed out of our locker room. As I walked out the door, I was greeted by my mother and my three sisters: Iesha, Radesha, and Adrianna. I told them I was proud of them because they were not allowing anything to distract them from making good grades in school. I was honored to know how much they looked up to me, and they were following my lead. They were not allowing anything negative such as poverty, or adverse circumstances, to deter them from their dreams and goals in life. As usual, my mom was wearing her # 20 Clemson jersey. It was wonderful just seeing the smiles on all of their faces. As we walked out to our car, I was bombarded by kids wanting autographs. As was usual for me, I signed as many as I could even though I was exhausted. My family knew me well, so they just went ahead to get into the car and wait for me until I was finished.

After the season I was going through, seeing my family was just what I needed. Mom cooked her homemade spaghetti, and we enjoyed each other's company. There was lots of fun and laughter. They had planned to drive back home to Mobile around 7:00 pm that evening. When the time came for them to head back, I sighed. As they pulled out of the parking lot of my apartment building, there were smiles on their faces.

My mother shouted, "I love you!" out of the window as they drove off. I watched them until they were out of sight.

I tossed and turned most of that night. I was unable to rest comfortably because I knew my family was traveling down the dark highways. I always hated it when they drove home late at night, and I would have trouble sleeping whenever they were on the road. It did not matter if they were coming to Clemson or heading home, this was normal for me. But this night was especially troublesome, and I was worried more than usual. I was not able to lie still, and calling over and over again to make sure they were safe. I always prayed that God would give them traveling mercies. Usually God would give me peace, but tonight was very different. At around 10 o'clock that night, I made the last call to my mom before falling into a deep, troubled sleep.

Ring..Ring.

I had just played a full game earlier that day, and I was dog-tired. There was no way I was getting up for that call. I simply rolled over and face the wall, away from the ringing phone. I never even glanced at the caller ID. I was sleeping very heavily, but I could hear the phone bringing repeatedly. They came one call after the other, but I was still unresponsive. I just tossed and turned in response to the ringing sound. When the phone rang the fourth time, I was awake enough that I decided to answer it. The caller ID said that the call was coming from an unknown number.

When I looked at the caller ID, I thought to myself, "is a bill collector really calling this late?"

It was obvious I was not thinking clearly. From my past experience, I never answered when it was an unknown number. Usually it was just someone you did not want to talk to, like a bill collector. Since we had often struggled financially, I was very familiar with that type of phone call. And they always seem to come at the most inopportune times. The lateness of the hour should have alerted me it was not a bill collector, but I was just that tired.

I answered reluctantly, and heard "Hello, Mr. Maye this is Officer..."

I instantly sat straight up in the bed. Despite how tired I was, I was now wide-awake. I was so shocked; I did not even get the officer's name. I started panicking, "What happened now?"

"I am calling on behalf of your family," my heart stopped, and I did not know what to expect.

I shouted, "Please, No! Tell me it is not so!"

I was crying, and thinking the worst. Tears were streaming down my face, and I did not know what happened to my family. All I could remember was them waving goodbye to me out of the car window. I needed to hear that they were fine. I tried to gather myself, but I knew I could not breathe again until the officer answered my questions. I had prayed so hard for their safe return home, and now I was hanging on the officer's every word.

In my heart, I said a silent prayer, "Lord, please let them be all right."

I had lost my father at a young age, and I had recently lost my best friend. I could not lose my mother and my sisters too. My heart could just not take that.

The officer's next words brought me the peace I had just prayed for. He said, "Mr. Maye, your family is fine. They just wanted me to give you a call because their phones were thrown from the car."

I was really confused now, and standing up in my room trying to make sense of the situation.

I said to the officer, "You first said they were fine, right? Now, you are saying that their phones were thrown from the car?"

The officer quickly responded, "Your family is safe. An 18-wheeler swerved out of its lane and into the one they were in. To avoid being hit by the truck, your mother swerved, and ended up rolling over. But for the most part, they are okay. The accident could have been much worse."

The way in which the officer described the accident to me made me appreciate God's grace and protection. They could have been dead. I was able to speak with each of them, and it was good to hear their voices. I was totally relieved. The thought of losing my family in an automobile accident was unimaginable, especially since they were traveling because of me. Guilt would have completely taken over my life. The accident frightened me severely, and afterwards I began to think about transferring to another school for my senior year, to be closer to my family. But this accident itself was not a strong enough motive for me to leave Clemson at that time. This had certainly been a season of setbacks, tragedies and heartbreak.

The next week we traveled to Tallahassee to play Florida State. Florida State was only about four hours from my hometown, so I had a crowd at that game that included my mom and dad, my sisters, aunt Ruben, uncle Mike, cousin Mustafa, cousin Jeremy, and a few of my sisters' friends. I was excited to see all of them at the game, but after the accident the previous week, I was worried about their safety driving to the game and back home. The night before the game, I could not sleep at all. I was up most of the night calling them, as they drove from Mobile to Tallahassee. I had to be sure they were safe. Worrying about my family traveling the highways to watch me play football began to affect my performance on the field. I was not getting enough sleep. My energy levels significantly decreased, and I often felt like I was in a fog. Despite my fatigue, I was excited about playing at Doak Campbell Stadium. I had heard about playing there, and I now had the opportunity to experience first-hand how amazing game day could be there. Clemson and Florida State games were always competitive and were some of the best games the ACC had to offer. This game got me excited. My feelings before kickoff were similar to those games we played against Auburn and Alabama. And I wanted to win. It would be especially extraordinary because we were going against them in their home environment and they definitely had the home field advantage.

We kicked off to Florida State. On the first possession of the game, I made a diving tackle on one of Florida State's running backs in the backfield. Boom! I caught a direct hit to the head from the hip of Dequan Bowers, and was knocked out cold. I felt like I had caught a right hook from Floyd Mayweather. I remembered everything that happened in the play, but due to precautions taken by our training staff, I was sidelined and not allowed to return to the game. Again, I had to watch as my teammates played. The events that had taken place this season changed me. Spending so much time on the sidelines, after having such a promising first two years, affected me mentally. Inside, I was hurting.

The NCAA has a rule that if you sustain a concussion in a game, you had to sit out the next week. This meant that again I would be on the sidelines when the team traveled to Winston-Salem, North Carolina to play Wake Forest. I was extremely discouraged. I felt I had been on the sideline more this season than I had played on the gridiron. For encouragement, I went to visit one of my friends in North Carolina, who lived about an hour away from Clemson. Since I could not travel with the team, I figured I would support them in spirit and be in the same state. Thinking about it now, I find it a little funny because I guess I have always been a team player.

I returned to the action just before our rivalry game against South Carolina. Earlier in the week, I had received even more devastating news. I found out that one of the most important women in my life was facing a battle of her own. I found out that my grandmother had been diagnosed with congestive heart failure. As soon as I got this information, I wanted to go home immediately. This news helped me decide what my future would be. I knew I would either transfer to another school to be closer to home, or I would enter the NFL draft. With that decision made, I decided to just enjoy the rest of the season with my teammates. For the last four years, they had become my brothers through blood, sweat, and tears.

In spite of all the negative things that had happened, I found it amazing that I had 50 tackles on the season. I led the team and the ACC in tackles, despite missing so much playing time. My mom is the one who called me with the news. I knew that my grandmother was in the hospital, instructing my family not to tell me. I knew my grandma wanted me to stay for the game. She always wanted what was best for the people that she loved, and wanted to lift them up so much that sometimes, she appeared invisible. I got a chance to talk with her that day, and she did just what I expected she would. She told me to be there with my team and that she would be watching from her hospital bed.

I did not tell anyone outside of my family about my decision to either transfer or enter the NFL draft, depending on my draft grade at the conclusion of the season. It was bittersweet knowing that my game against South Carolina would be the last one I played in the Valley. For the South Carolina game, I had two things I wanted to accomplish. First, I wanted to beat South Carolina. And, just prior to the game, I had made the decision to honor my teammate Scotty Cooper.

Scotty could not play due to a neck injury. Just as I had done when I wore the number 17 jersey in order to lift up my other teammate, I needed to do something for him too. I did not do these types of things to bring honor to me; I just wanted to let my teammates know how important they were to the team, and to me. I wanted them to understand that their sacrifices did not go unnoticed. I also wanted to make sure my teammates were honored. Scotty and Stanly were both four-star linebackers for Clemson. I had a personal relationship with those guys, because we were all brought in during the same recruiting class.

As I approached the Tiger Walk, I wanted to soak everything in: the fans, the chants, even the smell from the tailgates that made me hungry. As I made my way through the Tiger Walk for the last time, I reflected on all of the times I had done that through my previous seasons. Those were precious memories for me. In spite of the number of injuries I had sustained, I had started in 33 games as a Clemson Tiger. As we entered the door to the facility, I remembered my official visit. It seemed like just yesterday when I walked into the door for the first time, and decided to make Clemson University my home. The atmosphere in the locker room was calm, and my teammates had on their game faces. I went out early to walk on the field before getting dressed for warm-ups. It was a calm, cool night. I found myself just staring out at "The Hill" in the distance, and thinking about how Clemson had given me the chance to be great. They had given me a chance when no other colleges seem to give me a second look.

After a very emotional, upbeat pre-game speech from Coach Swinney, the team loaded the buses. I knew this would be my last ride. As I rode with the guys on the bus for the last time, the team called on me to perform my chant. The chant was my way to get everybody pumped up, and ready to play as we rode the bus.

"What time is it?" I would say.

"Game time," the team would reply.

I would repeat, "What time is it?"

They would reply again, "Game time!"

I continued, "Any dogs?"

Then my teammates would bark. We would do this several times. This was the chant I had learned from my mentor, Ray Lewis. By this time, we were getting off the bus and ready to walk through the shiny gates that sat in front of the rock. I had the #44 jersey on. My heart was pumping hard as I stood at the top of "The Hill," soaking in every minute. I saw thousands of fans screaming and hollering, dressed in all orange. Tonight I focused on just having fun playing football. I would not worry about winning or losing. I just wanted to run free, and enjoy the Valley for the last time. It would have been even more special if we had come away with a victory, but I was happy. I had accomplished my mission, and I was a starter for three great years. I was a part of the Clemson University family.

After the season, I submitted my papers to the NFL league office. I received a good enough grade that I considered entering the draft. I went back and forth on the issue, until the last day for juniors to declare. I decided that I was not going to enter the draft. I had made a promise to my mother earlier in my career that I would get my degree, and I was only one semester away from graduating. Graduating would be a huge accomplishment. No one in my family had ever earned a degree from a four-year college or university. I felt that, not only did I deserve to graduate after all of my hard work in the classroom and on the football field, but I owed it to the kids from my community. I could serve as a role model. I wanted them to see that if I could do it, they could do it too.

Instead of entering the NFL Draft, I decided to transfer after graduation. I desired to get closer to home where I could visit my sick grandmother. When I was released from the team, I received calls from Auburn, Texas A&M, Mississippi State, Kentucky, Florida, and many others. Out of respect, I would not talk to anyone including the media, until I had spoken to my team. I had Coach Swinney call a players-only meeting for me. I was honored that every player showed up and they understood my situation.

As I stood in front of my Clemson teammates, every set of eyes were locked on me, listening to what I had to say. I was humbled and grateful for the time I spent with such a classy group of men. I thought maybe some would be bitter or feel betrayed, but they understood. My last memory was the hugs and encouragement I received afterwards.

Later that month I took visits to Kentucky and Mississippi State. I know everyone was like Kentucky? Why? He said he wanted to get closer to home. The reason for the visit to Kentucky is that we had family in the area. I did not know if my grandma would have to go there or not. After taking both visits, I decided to sign with Dan Mullen and the Bulldogs. My four years at Clemson had made me a man. I was ready for whatever would come in Starkville.

My season at Mississippi State University turned out to be one of the most defining moments of my life. There was no way to avoid set- backs, tragedy, and hardships. I learned through experiences that when these things come into my life, not to run. It is important to face them head on. Chose to run toward them and persevere through them. At the end of the day, you will have developed character. As the Scripture says God does not give us a spirit of fear, but of love, peace, and a sound mind.

Throughout my years at Clemson, these words were always with me. I will always cherish my time at Clemson University.

My last game in Death Valley vs South Carolina.
Honoring teammate Scotty Copper by wearing #44.

My last game as a Clemson Tiger.
Meineke Car Bowl vs South Florida.

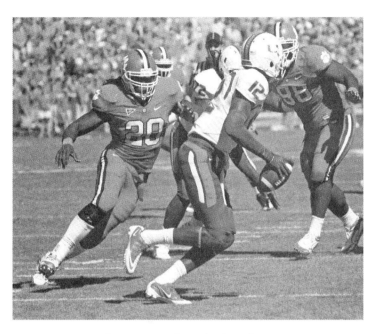

Always was fun playing the U.

11

RISE FROM THE ASHES

*"The Phoenix hope, can wing her through the desert skies, and
still defying fortune's spite; revive from ashes and rise."*

Miquel de Carvantes Saavedra

I n the spring of 2011, the week before graduation, I made one of the toughest decisions in my life. I elected to transfer from Clemson to Mississippi State University. It was my senior season. For four years, I had shared blood, sweat, and tears with my teammates. We had celebrated victories and lamented over defeats. Clemson had been my home away from home, and leaving was very painful for me. Despite the difficulty of this decision, it was one that had to be made. I understand priorities and the standard order of things: life, faith, family, football. Following these tenants is how I run my life. No matter what the outcome was, after I made a decision as long as I stuck to my rule, I was at peace. Many questioned my decision, but there were many right reasons for the transfer. These reasons were bigger than my grandmother's diagnosis of congestive heart failure, though she means the world to me. As a Clemson Football player, I had fulfilled my duties to the team. I had been a great citizen and conducted myself as a gentleman. I managed myself with class and dignity on and off the field. I gave back to the Clemson community.

I had tried to be a great teammate and I think I represented Clemson in a most positive manner; the way it should be.

Once finals ended and after many days of packing and cleaning my apartment, the day finally came for me to leave Clemson. I wish I could tell you that this was just another 4-year college graduate moving back home story, but sadly I cannot. Because of my connection to the people there, the situation was much harder. My decision gave me an opportunity to see how committed to my success Clemson University really was, and showed me how caring the people of the community truly are. Leaving Clemson felt as if I were leaving behind a family that had adopted me, cared for me, and loved me. I had built a strong bond with each and every one of my teammates and coaches. They had developed a respect for me as a man and a player because they knew I spoke from the heart when I talked. They will never know what their support really meant because there are not enough words to say how much they touched me.

On the last night, as I lay in my bed, which was the only thing left unpacked in my apartment, many thoughts ran through my head. I had tried to get out of bed once, but all I managed to do was make a mess and knock boxes over. Once, I actually fell out of the bed. I was physically and emotionally drained. I had been up all night packing things and failed to organize the boxes as I should have. Obviously football players, a room full of moving boxes, and a bed do not make for a good combination. I was paying for it now, as I lay face first on my apartment floor. I had to laugh at myself because I quickly turned my head looking around the room to make sure no one saw me. I guess the funniest thing about this is that I knew I lived alone, but I naturally looked anyway. It did not matter where you were, if you tripped or stumbled over something, it was sure to draw some laughs and jokes from my teammates. Trust me, when you are around a bunch of other players, you are always looking to see who saw you do something like that. You will never hear the end of it if they do. They say stuff like "do you remember when this person did" this or that? I have been on the giving and receiving end of those comments before. I am guessing when they read this, they will say it again. If the shoe were on the other foot, I know I would.

After scraping myself up off the floor, I went into the bathroom for my normal early morning routine. I brushed my teeth, and washed my face. After my morning clean up, my stomach started to growl, so I went to my refrigerator. But when I opened the door, to my surprise, it was completely empty. I rushed back into my bedroom, grabbed my cellphone, and called my friend Monesha, a member of the volleyball team. She had come over the previous night to help me clean up. So I called her at 6:30 in the morning.

Ring... Ring.... Ring....

She answered sleepily.

"Morning Mo," I said in a low voice, trying not to completely wake her up.

She responded in a weak, whispering manner, "Yes...LaCosta," which is what she called me, referring to my middle name.

"What happened to all the food that was in the fridge?" I asked.

The phone then grew silent before she responded, "Ummm... I threw it all in the trash can. I figured you did not need it any more since you are leaving us today."

Her response cut my heart into a thousand pieces.

I smiled, "Dang Mo, you could have dropped that news a little lighter on me."

Throughout our conversation, I reflect on all of the friendships and memories that I had made while at Clemson. As our conversation went on I reflected on the memories that I had made at Clemson. I knew that these would sing be distant memories, and it pained my heart.

She laughed and concluded, "Well it's the truth. I will be over later to say good bye."

"Okay, I said, "thanks again for all the help."

After hanging up the phone, I was still hungry and really needed to eat something. My parents were on their way to Clemson with my cousin Terrance, to help me move my things back to Mobile. A quick phone call confirmed that they were still about four hours away in Montgomery. Since I knew there was no need to rush, I went over to Paul's diner. Paul's diner was a small dining hall that had the best home cooking in Clemson. You would have never known based on the look of the place, but it was a place I loved. Many of my team- mates and I had eaten many of the meals at Paul's diner. The food was always amazing. When I ate dinner there, I would eat the prime rib eye steak, mashed potatoes, collard greens, rolls, and strawberry shortcake. But since it was breakfast, I ordered some of my favorite: Grits, eggs, sausage, with two slices of toast topped off with grape jelly. I was a regular there, and I had spent many hours in this place talking to fans and signing autographs.

I got a call from my mom about two hours later.

"We are in Atlanta, and should be there shortly. Make sure your things are ready so we can get back on the road quickly."

Mom did not know I had been up all night packing and arranging boxes so that they were ready to be loaded on the truck as soon as they arrived. My mom has always been a neat freak, so I knew that it did not matter that I had everything packed. She was going to spend time wiping and cleaning everything anyways. I was exhausted by this time, and ready to get on the road. I knew it was going to take some convincing on my part to persuade Mom to leave things the way they were until we returned to my apartment for graduation.

I was exhausted so I laid down on my floor, surrounded by my boxes, until they arrived.

The next thing I knew, I heard my mom yelling, "We are outside."

The feelings of guilt and exhaustion quickly left me when I heard my mom. Any opportunity to see my family was special to me, and always picked up my spirits. My mom is finally here I thought. I was going home for a few days, only to return in time for my graduation from Clemson University.

Moving my stuff back home went smoothly. My dad Osben, my cousin Terrance, teammate Carlton Lewis, and I loaded the Dodge Ram truck in about 45 minutes. Mom must have been very excited to see me, because she did not try to clean up everything. It was a little strange for her.

After we finished loading my things onto the truck, we prepared for the drive back to Mobile. I normally would have asked my mom to ride with me in my car, but this time I needed some time alone. I knew I needed to do something. My heart was heavy. I started my car and began to drive to the security gates and out of the Harts Cove Apartments. I was driving towards the interstate. I decided to take the long way, so I could pass by the stadium. Passing by Death Valley always gave me an adrenaline rush.

I had almost completely passed by the stadium, before I turned around to go back. I did not understand why I made this detour. I thought to myself, people are going to really think I am crazy, as I sat in my car, staring at the empty stadium. Someone else looking through these gates at the same time as me would not have seen any- thing, but to me the stadium was not empty. I could see the 80,000 fans, I could hear people yelling, "Fight Tigers! Fight Tigers! Fight! Fight! Fight!" And I could smell the sweat of me and my team- mates, as we battled our opponents on the gridiron. For me, Death Valley would never be empty because it would always have part of my heart in it.

There was calmness over my body, and I found peace in this deci- sion. I got out of my car and walked towards the gates. These gates were usually locked, but by some miracle of God, they were open. My knees were knocking and I became weak. I knew that this was possibly the last time I would see Death Valley. I thought of the love that I had for Clemson University for granting me an opportunity to achieve my dreams. I was thankful for the people who coached me on and off the field. I had obtained a degree and I was pleased. I had dreamed of accomplishing this and it was now a reality. I wanted to personally thank God.

With my hand on the rock, I prayed a silent prayer. This prayer would change my life forever. *"Lord, thank you for allowing me to persevere and defeat all the odds that have presented themselves since childhood. Now because of your grace and faithfulness to me in my family, I am a week from destroying those generational curses and giving hope to those that will follow me. I stand hum- bled before you."*

By this time a cool breeze grazed my forehead. Knowing that it was the spirit of God, I continued as tears ran down the side of my face, *"I want to thank you for the great people at Clemson for giving me an opportunity to be great, not only on the field, but in life, in the class, and in the community. As I go forth, no matter what happens in my future, I understand that you have been good to me. I, bringing nothing, allowed you to turn me into something special."*

After saying those words I turned around and made my way back to my car. Even though I knew I was returning for graduation, this emotional moment with the man upstairs could not be replaced. I had finally found peace with my decision to transfer, and play my senior year at Mississippi State. I understood that if no one else knew, God knew my situation, that was all that mattered.

At home, I found myself fighting back emotions. I played board games with my family to relax. Spending time with my family made me reflect on how good God had been to us. He had blessed us be- yond measure. I thought of the two-bedroom shack we once lived in. I thought of how times like this made the sounds of sirens and gunshots seem trivial. Laughing and enjoying each other was a blessing, and I cherished it.

The week at home passed quickly, and my Clemson Graduation was to be on Friday May 13th. On Thursday, we loaded up a 15-passenger van with family members. We looked like a modern day Brady Bunch. This trip with my family was exciting. We had on board my Uncle Sam and Aunt Cathy. These two looked like twins, and loved to be around each other. They joked with each other all of the time, too. Their interaction provided entertainment for us the entire trip, and we traveled the whole way without any complaints. Having my family with me for graduation meant the world to me. The love and support they had shown me during this endeavor made all the trials and tribulations worthwhile.

Though we stopped often to allow my elderly grandma to stretch her legs, it was not long before we were pulling into Clemson. My family members had always been there for me on my biggest days, and this was no exception. It was especially important to me to see my elderly grandma make this sacrifice in her condition. It helped my family and I understand just how special this day was.

When we arrived at my empty apartment, we were all exhausted. My small three-bedroom apartment was covered with blowup mat- tresses and people sleeping on pallets. It reminded me of the way we had shared that small bedroom when I was younger. I sighed with contentment as I turned off the lights, but I didn't go to sleep right away. I was too excited about what would take place the next day. Just as I was about to fall asleep, the sound of someone snoring woke me up. Though many people would have been frus- trated, this sound did not bother me. My family was with me and I was on cloud nine.

When the restless night turned to bright, sunny morning, I rose to the sound of the chirping birds. It was about 8am and every- one, except my grandmother was still sleeping. I stood looking in amazement at my grandmother, who had gotten up and prepared breakfast. The apartment smelled like a buffet. My mouth watered as I washed my face and prepared myself. All I could think about was: homemade butter biscuits, bacon, sausage, grits and spend- ing this day with my family.

I went into the kitchen and greeted my grandmother warmly. She always had a message for me. And this morning was one of the most special. She ordered me to sit down in this plastic, green chair that I had left behind. While everyone else was sleeping away, my grandmother and I just shared a special moment in the kitchen of that small apartment alone.

She started talking in her soft, sweet voice, "Words cannot express how proud I am of you to see you defeat the odds and accomplish something no one else in our family has ever done. The standard that you have set has given all of the kids, and even some of the adults, a different mindset. It has given them hope that if they dare to dream it, they can achieve it."

I had never seen my grandma cry before. No matter what happened, she had always been a rock for our family. Now as she spoke with me and I looked into her dull blue eyes, I could see the tears that she was fighting back.

Then, she continued, "When you left for college on that first day, I told you to shock the world. But you not only reached that goal, you exceeded it. I promised you then, if I had breath in my body, I was going to be here for this ceremony because I know the struggle behind your story. As I watched you get into all kinds of trouble as a child, I still knew that God had his hand on you. I knew that you were special. I pray that you continue to trust him and let him guide you down life's path, throughout the rest of your life's journey."

I knew the day would be an emotional one. I expected Mom to cry a lot, but I was not expecting to start this day off with words from my grandma, as she sat in that small kitchen with tears in her eyes. The word she said took me back to a conversation we had before. It was when I first found out that she was sick. I was sitting alone in my Hart's Cove apartment in Clemson, when she promised me that, when I graduated, she would be there. I remembered the tears that rushed down my face and, even though no one else was there, I still tried to fight back the tears because of the sentiments behind each and every word. You see, the doctors had instructed her that she was just too sick and weak for that long of a journey, but she was determined to see with her own eyes, the first person in our family or from our small, tightknit community, walk across that stage and receive their college diploma. With her weary eyes, she had watched generation after generation fall under the curse of not valuing their education. Many just did not value what a degree meant, and many even dropped out. I knew of the sacrifices both she and my mom had made to get me this far, and their sacrifices were what drove me. They pushed me to be the best I could be in any situation, from my spiritual life, to the gridiron, and especially in the classroom. I knew that I didn't just want my diploma; I aspired to set an example for my family. I wanted more, and today was the day. I was not only earning my degree, but I was graduating with distinction; I was graduating Cum Laude. What made it even more special was that I knew that my grandmother was going to share this day with me. I had worked so very hard for everything I had received in my life, but I can't take all the credit because it was not mine to take. The real credit belongs to God, my family, and everyone else who had supported me through the years.

An event of this magnitude was much bigger than me as an individual. This event was also for the kids still living in neighborhoods just like mine that had no strength to go after their dreams anymore, because they were exhausted with just struggling to survive day to day. They have no hope for a better tomorrow. I wanted my degree to show them that they can get an education too. This event was for the families in my community that felt they could never escape the struggle of poverty. This event was for those who did not have faith, for those who stopped praying and believing that their prayers would never be answered. It is for those who did not believe that hard work could change their lives forever. I wanted people in my neighborhood to know that I walked those same lonely streets of desperation with dreams that soon faded, becoming only a distant fairy tale, and that fairy tales are only something you see in movies or read in books. Despite all the obstacles that came along this journey, I knew this day would come.

As a young child I had heard stories about individuals choosing to take a different road, and how it could provide hope and inspiration to many. The stories captivated me and I realized that this person was soon to become me. Surrounded by peer pressure, violence, and poverty, I had dared to dream of this moment since I was 8 years old. I wanted to create a different way of acquiring success. My way was inspired by scripture, and meant success without taking any shortcuts; it meant achievement through hard work, and focus. I did not understand at the time where God was taking me, but the destination was as clear to me as a polished, flawless diamond. My graduation and earning my degree is all about guidance, perseverance and courage to chase greatness, in an effort to leave a legacy. And my hope, well that is simple. I hope my achievement may inspire others for generations and generations to come.

Because Clemson University had so many students, graduation ceremonies were broken into two segments; a 9:30 ceremony and a 3:30 ceremony. Fortunately, I was in the afternoon ceremony. I had lived with girls all my life, and knew that the extra time would also be beneficial for everybody. I knew my sisters and mom usually took at least one hour each to bathe, put on makeup and dress.

After breakfast, time seem to stand still. I was so excited about today's events, and it just seemed to take forever. Many friends came over to congratulate me and take pictures. One of the most special visits was that of Scott Carpenter, and his wife. Scott was a very spiritual person that I had met and built a strong bond with after he was the keynote speaker at one of our game day services during my sophomore year. This guy was truly a blessing to me. He was direct yet tactful. I respected him because he shot straight when it came to what the Bible says.

Throughout my career at Clemson, he would drive down from his home in Greenville to meet with me, and mentor me. He was a friend and provided a light in some of my darkest hours. He was like a proud, spiritual father. He was smiling from ear to ear as he saw me now, dressed in black dress pants, an orange shirt, striped dark and light orange tie, standing in the living room. With his visit, I knew it was close to the time--time to go to Little John Basketball Arena, the location for the graduation ceremony!

I could not sit still and I remember going from room to room pacing. I was feeding off the excitement in that small apartment and I knew that soon, I would be walking across that stage. I was nervous. I was biting my nails. I nearly bit them down to the quick, I was so nervous. The anticipation of the graduation ceremony reminded me a lot of a locker room on game day.

The room went quiet and then, my mom shouted, "Okay, it is time to head that way."

After standing around my apartment for hours taking pictures with my cap and gown on, my family and I loaded the van and went to the arena. We left around noon. We wanted to get there early, so we could get good parking spots. We also wanted to beat the crowds, so we could get my grandma seated quickly. The closer we got to Little John, the more my heart pounded.

As I rode along, I could not help but think about the people who told me this moment would never happen. I also thought about my friends, many of whom were dead or in jail. I thought about the route I had chosen. I thought of how powerful God is, and how he had blessed me. I had to thank him for my family, a family who believed in my dreams and help me achieve them.

As we made the last turn into the Coliseum parking lot, I was quiet. But I also knew there was a huge smile on my face as I got out of the van. After I was dropped off at the front entrance, I walked into the arena to where the teachers, advisors, and staff members were organizing students by their names and majors. I held my head high when they announced my name, and made my way to my place in line. We stood for hours waiting for all students to get in order. Everyone was excited about graduation. I do not know if it meant more to me or not, this moment was extremely important to all of us, but the fact that I achieved this feat, despite my struggles, made it more meaningful. It had been a huge weight for me to carry, wanting this for my family and my community, but now that weight had lifted.

After all the graduates were lined up, we started our walk through the glass doors of the Coliseum. We went outside to a beautiful, breezy, sunny afternoon. We walked until we came up to a huge door that separated us from the noisy, cheering crowd that awaited our entrance. I took a deep breath before we walked out. I wondered if I would finally wake up, and find that this all was a dream.

As we entered the arena, there were loud cheers from the crowd. It was now happening, for real. I would become the first in my family to get a college degree. Doors were now going to be opened. My success would allow others to see that they can step out on faith to achieve something. I understood how some miss out on their opportunity because of fear of failure. I do not believe in mistakes. I believe in God. God granted each of us an opportunity when he sent Jesus to die for our sins on Calvary. Many of us forget about our spirit within. We forget about God when things are challenging, instead of deciding to trust in the Word. When we dig deep within ourselves and decide we are going to go get it no matter what obstacles or setbacks come our way, great things can and will happen. There were times when I fell on my face, times when my heart was broken, and times I would have rather been somewhere else during this journey. Obtaining a college degree was once the last thing on my mind, yet because of the grace of God and special relationships with people, my struggles became evidence of God's power.

As I walked with my graduating class to my seat, I thought about how different my life would be if I had chosen another route. I did not commit any serious crimes in my youth, but I was on the edge of the criminal fraternity, and could have easily been another brother in jail. My eyes searched the inside of the arena. There were thousands of people in this place. There were speechmakers, but I could not concentrate on their messages of hope and the future. I was busy trying to locate my family amidst the crowd. People were packed in so close together that they blended in. I could not find Mom, but I located my grandma and aunt. They were seated far out in the stands behind the stage. They had gotten separated from the rest of my family when the others were parking the van. I could see my aunt going back and forth with my grandma trying to point me out.

She would point and then look to my grandma to ask the question, "Do you see him?"

I tried to help by simply looking in their direction, and by waving my hands. I knew people were wondering why I was waving my hand in the middle of the speeches, but I was so excited I did not care what anybody thought. As the speeches came to an end, we were instructed, row-by-row to stand, and were escorted toward the side ramp to go onto the stage. Filled with mix emotions, I looked around still searching for Mom. I was holding back tears when I finally spotted my Mom and the rest of my family sitting behind us, near the top of the arena. Mom was proud and crying crocodile tears.

The closer I got to the stage, the bigger my astonishment became. In the stands was Kila Rumph, the wife of Coach Rumph, and she had her two sons with her. They had driven down from Tuscaloosa, Alabama to attend my graduation. Coach Rumph had taken a job at the University of Alabama, as the defensive line coach. Kila and Coach Rumph had been my parents away from home when I attended Clemson.

Walking toward that stage graduation day was special because I believed that every person that had something to do with my success was in attendance. When I looked to my left, as I waited for our row to be called, I saw Ms. Amy and her two sons Will and Jack. Ms. Amy, an elementary teacher in South Carolina, had presented me with multiple opportunities to give back to young people. She encouraged me to come to school events and speak to her class. Ms. Amy was dependable and trustworthy. She made things happen.

I took another deep breath and finally, I was up with everyone on my row getting ready to make that walk on the stage. In a straight line, we waited on the side of the stage, next to the ramp. This was the most nervous I had ever been in my life. There were four steps on the ramp leading to the stage. These four steps I was taking to the stage were not only for me, but for the kids in my community that had little or no faith. I knew if I could do it, they could do it too. These steps were taken for the families that gave up and had little or no hope. These steps were taken for the youth that had no self-esteem. I took these steps for anyone being told they "cannot," "could not," "would not," and for those who did not understand what hard work and dedication produced. As I waited at the bottom before taking the first step onto the ramp, I envisioned all four of these groups joining hands and getting ready to make this walk with me. It was not about me; it was about all of us. Since childhood, I have carried with me the chains that held my community down and created an oppressed atmosphere with no hope. I wore these chains in hopes of changing this mind and breaking the chains. I thanked God again, for using me. He chose and equipped me mentally for this battle. God, through the game of football, cut and polished me so I could be used to change the mindset of those with no hope, to be an example of how dreams come true, and to show that with God, we can overcome anything poverty, drugs, violence, and peer pressure could bring our way.

As I took the first step of the ramp, I envisioned the shackles around my body rattling and swinging back and forth. There were three graduates in front of me. I made the second step and could feel the shackles loosen a little. I took the third step and the burden that haunted generations from not getting an education was gone. One step left and I am now standing at the top of the ramp exposed to everyone in the arena. To my right was the Board of Trustees, who had recognized my academic achievements. For about ten seconds, I took in the significance of what this graduation ceremony meant. I took a final glance at my family, turned and looked at my grandma and aunt, and exhaled. The best thing that could happen in my life was happening at that moment.

I heard my name called, "Brandon Maye, Cum Laude."

Before coming to Clemson, I had made a promise to my mom that I would not only work hard and do well in classes, but I would graduate with honors. It was challenging, but I kept my promise. As I walked towards President Barker standing with my degree in his hand, I could finally see the shackles being released from my body, leaving only black ashes covering the white stage floor, and creating a different mindset for those who did not believe in the dream. As I continued my walk, emotions took over my body and tears ran down my face. Though I have dreams of one day walking on the stage at the NFL Draft, and holding up a team jersey, I know only a few get that chance. The emotions that I had this graduation day are just as powerful, if not more so. I think that way because getting signed by an NFL team would be my accomplishment, but this accomplishment was truly a team effort. And I knew they were all there in Little John Coliseum with me, either in body or in spirit.

When I reached the top of the exit ramp, I looked up at my grandma one more time. She was soaking it all in. My mom had made her way to the stage to capture pictures of this moment. With the graduation directors flagging me to hurry off the stage, I posed constantly holding up my degree for all to see. I wanted everyone to capture this picture. I had achieved something no man could ever take from me, that would give me pathways to be successful in life beyond my football career. As my mom took the picture, I glanced at my grandma. After all these years, we had survived homelessness, poverty, losing family members, setbacks, and many obstacles, yet this was the first time I saw her break down and cry. She tried to hide it, but I saw everything in her eyes and I treasured it.

The greatest moment of my life outside of getting the Master's degree a year later.

Words cannot express this moment with my family in the crowd.

12

ANOTHER STEP OF FAITH

"For I am confident of this very thing, that He who began a good work in you will perfect it until the day of Christ Jesus."

Philippians 1:6

After my graduation from Clemson, I knew I had to take another huge step of faith. I had prayed long and hard about my decision to either enter the draft, or to transfer during my senior playing season. I knew it would be a big adjustment for me, but my family was extremely supportive. The greatest comfort for me at that time came from my mom and dad, and my girlfriend Jennifer Johnson. Though I knew it would be hard, I also knew that this was the best thing for my family. I knew I would miss the coaches and my teammates at Clemson, but most of all, I would miss the fans.

A major area of concern for me was my football future. Because of my grandmother's illness, and other factors, I knew that it was best for me not to enter the NFL draft at that time, which that is why I decided to transfer. It was a big deal for a player that had as much success as I did at Clemson to transfer during his senior season.

Throughout the transfer process, I knew that several things needed to come together for me, as I chose where to finish my collegiate football career. First of all, whatever team I chose needed to be a fierce competitor in their conference. I knew I only had one year left to impress the NFL scouts. Because of my injuries, I knew I had to rack up some substantial numbers. Another factor I had to consider was the team's depth chart. To impress those NFL scouts, I had to make sure that I would have enough playing time to make a significant contribution to my new team. But the most important factor of all was how close it would be to home.

After being contacted by some of the nation's top programs, I decided to make official visits to Kentucky and Mississippi State. Both schools are in the SEC conference, and that would provide a new challenge for me. Both schools laid out the red carpet for me, and showed me ways that their programs could help me reach my NFL and Master's degree goals.

After making both visits, I sat down with my parents and we carefully weighed the pros and cons of both schools. I prayed a long time about my decision. I needed God to show me, which place was right for me to finish both my academic and college football careers. I knew that God did not bring me this far to fail me so I prayed for God's guidance, as I made one of the most important decisions of my life. God gave peace to me one night while lying in my bed praying.

A couple of weeks after my initial visit, my family and I came back to Mississippi State and had a sit-down meeting with Coach Mullen. We made the final decision in his office. My decision had nothing to do with what the coaches said in particular. I think it had more to do with the honesty shown to me by Head Coach Mullen, and Defensive Coordinator Coach Wilson. They told me that I could be the Ray Lewis type of leader they were looking for, but they did not sugarcoat things for me. They told me that the opportunity was there, but I would have to work hard from day one. They knew that with my hard work, dedication, and drive, that I could bring the experience of a veteran to their team. I knew this would be hard, but I accepted the challenge willingly. I know that God did not give within me a spirit of fear, but of power.

Like any other human, I had concerns. With me being such a vocal leader, I was concerned about how the players would react to me. Just like at Clemson, I knew I would have to earn the respect of the other players. With this being so late in my career, of course, there were also concerns that the scouts would question my character because of the transfer. Since I had been a three-year starter at Clemson, they may wonder if I just bailed because the times were tough, and I had to compete for playing time. Another main concern was that I would have to learn their playbook from cover to cover, in only two months. Though I eventually caught on, it was a struggle to erase the years of training by my Clemson coaches. I was also worried that I had missed much of camp with an injury. Coach Mullen explained to me what to expect from him and his staff and what they expected of me. Because all of my classes were online, it would be football, football, and more football, and of course I liked the sound of that.

Mississippi State was more of a blue-collar experience for me, from the head coach Dan Mullen, to the athletic director Mr. Strickland. I was very thankful for the opportunity and the faith they showed in me. Not only was it a risk for me and my career, but it was also a risk for them as well. They were willing to provide a full scholarship to a player who they knew would only be there for a short time.

One of the most important things that I remember about my time at Mississippi State was the training. It was very intense. The head strength coach, Coach Balis, had recently left the Florida Gators. He is very passionate about training, and had a specific style that I had never seen before.

When I looked around the weight room, I thought to myself, "What have I gotten myself into," and laughed.

My new strength coach was one of the toughest I had ever worked with. I really had not expected that their strength program would be life changing for me. After going through some of the stuff that we did during training camp, I felt that nothing in the real world could rattle me.

It didn't matter how many years I had played college football, or how many starts I had, I only knew now that I had to build a relationship with my new teammates. The game plan was to come in and be a leader, but I understood that there were a lot of guys that had paid a high price to be called a leader on this team. I knew I was the new guy. My plan was to show them that I had bought into the program, and could be a leader through my work ethic, commitment to film study, and doing extra things on the field. I knew I had my work cut out for me.

By week two, the team leaders took notice of my hard work ethic and vocal leadership. Among their leaders was junior cornerback Jonathan Banks, junior defensive and first-round draft pick Fletcher Cox, senior offensive lineman Quinton Salisbury, current Atlanta Falcons player Charles Mitchell, senior defensive back Wade Bonner, and running back and current Colts starter Vick Ballard. Eventually, I started to see that the players were starting to open up to me. Younger linebackers were starting to ask me more questions about the game. I took extra time to study film with them, and at the end of the first season, I had become a part of their family. All of the players were excited to have me as part of their team, from the first day to the last. I had learned a lot coming from one team to another, and I was amazed at how quickly and tightly our bond would grow. One of my closest friends that made the greatest impact on me during my time at Mississippi State was Brandon Wilson. He was a hard-working blue-collar guy, who was actually competing with me for my position. Even with me coming in, he was very helpful because he spent a lot of extra time helping me pick the play. Not only was he teaching me things, but he was always asking me questions and soaking up my knowledge. It made me think of iron sharpening iron, one man sharpens the other. That was the case with us. This guy just worked and worked, and then worked some more. He was always positive and supporting, and we eventually became co-starters after my injury. He showed me that life would be tough, and things will sometimes go against you, but if you stayed true to who you were, and continued to fight through the obstacles, the reward would be greater at the end. Throughout the whole season, I was only playing about 60%. With his determination to improve, and show other people they were wrong about him, he reminded me a lot of myself. He had been a walk on, but that never stopped him. He finished out the year as the fifth top tackler in the SEC. He and I often talk about how we were looked over by other schools, and we laugh about it now.

During the second week of camp after becoming a starter, I was injured again. It was tough on me as I watch the players practice, and I lost ground in the playbook. It seemed like maybe I had made the wrong decision after all.

As I battled through all the pain, game after game, I learned many new life lessons. Most of all I learned how to be a team player. I was so used to being a standout at Clemson, but here I was just one of the guys. I learned that tough situations don't always last, but tough people do.

I guess my most memorable time at Mississippi State was during the Music City Bowl. I had mixed emotions about that bowl game, because I had played there when I was at Clemson as well. My teammates from Clemson were heading to the Orange bowl. They all called me and joked with me that they were heading to the warm Miami weather, but I was heading to the cold weather of Nashville.

Many said to me, "enjoy the snow, while we are on South Beach."

In spite of this, I really enjoyed the ballgame. I did not tell anyone from a team that, before the game, I had to have a cortisone shot and I did not think I would be able to play from the pain that was in my Achilles at the time, but I sucked it up. I played through the pain. I played like it was my very last football game. The most memorable play for me came on this night, versus Wake Forest. It was fourth down and we needed a stop to close the game. I came off the edge on a blitz, and sacked the quarterback, which caused a fumble to end the game. It was so ironic to me because this was the exact same type of play I had made during my very first football game at the age of four. In spite of the fact that I was injured, and I had been gut checked during my senior season, I will never forget the look on my teammates and coaches faces as I ran to the bench with the ball in my hand.

Not only had this been a challenging year for me on the football field, it was hard in the classroom as well. I had so many things going on in my life. I had to have surgery, I was writing this book, and had many class assignments and tests to finish. I know that it was only God who gave me the strength to be able to do all of this during the late night hours. It was wearing my body down. I was only sleeping about three hours a night, but it was better for me to stay busy.

For someone who had made the All-ACC academic team, I was struggling. Taking online classes was vastly different for me, and I was not sure I would have the grades I needed to graduate. As soon as I found out, I ran into my mom's room to tell her. She started calling everybody. First she called my dad, who was very excited. I just remember my mom screaming, "Brandon got his Masters!"

I could hear him screaming on the other end of the call. He was so excited and proud of me. It was a very exciting day. So many didn't believe that it was possible for me to get the bachelor's degree, and now, here I was with a master's degree. I knew that God had opened another door for others to follow, and there were no limits when you put God first.

The hardest part of the last weeks of class was making up all of the work that I had missed during surgery. That had put me far behind, but I was able to go from a F to a B in the last days. I was at a loss for words, knowing that it would not be possible, if it was not for the Lord. All I could do was stand in the bathroom, and praise God. I could hear my sisters in the halls of our house screaming, as they went to my grandmother's room to tell her. They almost scared her to death with their shouting.

The first thing my mom and sisters did was run to the store to shop for food for my celebration. We had a huge family get together that night. Throughout the night, every time I looked at my mom, she had tears in her eyes.

Someone asked where are you going from here? Well I do not feel my work is done. I still feel that God has other important things for me to do. One day, I plan to be a great husband, father, and most importantly a servant for Christ. I felt fortunate, I had a dream to change the way others thought and believed, and by faith I realized my dream. I was able to show so many people that, no matter what you want in life, you can achieve it.

Well, this story is written now, and I plan to speak all over the country inspiring and motivating others through my words. What does my future hold? God only knows. But I intend to take it one day at a time, and set some new goals to continue to be an inspiration to others. I want to change people's lives and encourage as many people as I can through life's journey. God has been so good to me and my family, even when we really don't deserve it. I want to use my story as a platform that puts me in front of many people, who may be struggling. I want to tell them to never give up on their dreams. Though they may be in during a storm, eventually it will pass. I am here to tell them that the pain will only last for a moment, but if you have faith, you can do the impossible just like I did.

Playing my senior season through pain after injuring my achilles in camp.

Mississippi State football

Mississippi State vs Memphis

Before telling my story, I learned that diamond manufacturers analyze diamonds in the rough from an economic perspective. They want to know if they are going to get the maximum return on their investment. The process is much like recruiters looking for talent for their teams. They too want to be successful. The coaches at Clemson University and Mississippi State University saw my potential, and gave me the opportunity to shine on and off the football field. The coaches and administrators looked beyond my tattered clothes and tainted background.

What I want most is for people to analyze me from a spiritual perspective. I want to do my best to uphold the principles of Christ, and not allow his death on the cross to be in vain. God gives me the opportunity daily to confess my sins, repent of my sins, and receive forgiveness for my sins. Together with my family and friends, I have worked through sadness, disappointment, and pain. Negative thoughts were overcome with scripture, and God's Word always prevailed.

I, Brandon Maye, am a diamond in the rough. I have a kind word and soft smile. At first glance I appear quite ordinary. My true beauty is only realized through the cutting and polishing process of living the life God has called me to live. So far, that has meant overcoming trials, challenges, hardship, and death, yet I have no regrets. My life story is still being written, each and every day. But now, I know the importance of putting whole heartily my confidence in the Lord, allowing him to fight my battles. I pray that a return to the NFL is in God's plan for my future, but I understand now that if that's not the plan, he will install favor on whatever path he leads me. As I continue this journey, my goal is to allow my light to shine so that others are encouraged to persevere and achieve their dreams. Since I am not perfect, I will continue to fall short of God's glory but I will press forward on this earthly mission, working to show myself worthy to hear those sweet words, "Well done, my good and faithful servant," when this heart beats no more.

When someone tries to discourage you from pursuing your dreams, remember me...think of yourself as a diamond in the rough, pray often, and read Philippians 4:13 which states...

"I can do all things through Christ which strengthens me."

BOOK
BRANDON

Looking for a Motivational Speaker to ignite your company, school, non-profit organization, church, athletic team or youth events? Brandon knows what it takes to attain and sustain success and overcome odds in the areas of Sports, Education and Business.Brandon shares encouraging and heartfelt messages that are sure to take the lives of your listeners to the next level. Book Brandon for your next event

For Booking Please Contact:
ParExBooking@gmail.com

For Media Request Contact:
Jennifer@IconMediaGroup.us

CONNECT
With BRANDON

🐦 @bmaye9

📘 Facebook.com/Brandonlmaye.com

📷 bmaye251

🖥 www.brandonmaye.com

@ Brandonmayefanmail@gmail.com

SPIRIT REIGN
PUBLISHING
A Division of Spirit Reign Communications